I0491023

ART BOOKS

FROM CRESCENT MOON PUBLISHING

Leonardo da Vinci
by James Pearson

Early Netherlandish Painting
by Rosalind Mutter

Piero della Francesca
by Naomi Haskell

Giovanni Bellini
by Julia Davis

Eric Gill: Nuptials of God
by Anthony Hoyland

Minimal Art and Artists In the 1960s and After
by Laura Garrard

Postwar Art
by George Knighton

Vincent van Gogh: Visionary Landscapes
by Stuart Morris

Max Beckmann
by Stuart Morris

Egon Schiele: Sex and Death in Purple Stockings
by D. Simon Eade

Mark Rothko: The Art of Transcendence
by Julia Davis

Jasper Johns
by L.M. Poole

Brice Marden
by Laura Garrard

Frank Stella: American Abstract Artist
by James Pearson

The Light Eternal: J.M.W. Turner
by Jeremy Mark Robinson

Maurice Sendak and the Art of Children's Book Illustration
by L.M. Poole

Sex in Art: Pornography and Pleasure in Painting and Sculpture
by Cassidy Hughes

Glorification: Religious Abstraction
In Renaissance and 20th Century Painting
by Jeremy Mark Robinson

The Art of Andy Goldsworthy
by William Malpas

Andy Goldsworthy: Touching Nature
by William Malpas

Andy Goldsworthy In Close-Up
by William Malpas

The Art of Richard Long
by William Malpas

Constantin Brancusi: Sculpting the Essence of Things
by James Pearson

Alison Wilding: The Embrace of Sculpture
by Susan Quinnell

The Erotic Object: Sexuality in Sculpture
From Prehistory to the Present Day
by Susan Quinnell

Land Art: A Complete Guide to Landscape, Environmental,
Earthworks, Nature, Sculpture and Installation Art
by William Malpas

Land Art In Close-Up
by William Malpas

Colourfield Painting: Minimal, Cool, Hard Edge, Serial
and Post-Painterly Abstract Art From the Sixties to the Present
by Laura Garrard

Bellini
By Jennie Ellis Keysor

The Life of Michelangelo Buonarroti
By John Addington Symonds

Dante Gabriel Rossetti
By Esther Wood

Rodin: The Man and His Art
Edited by Judith Cladel

Rodin
By Rainer Maria Rilke

Fra Angelico
By James Mason

The Madonna In Art
By Estelle Hurll

The Venetian School of Painting
By Evelyn Phillipps

Boucher
By Haldane McFall

Leonardo da Vinci
By Maurice Brockwell

Famous European Painters
By Sarah Bolton

Delacroix
By Paul Konody

HANS MEMLING

HANS MEMLING

BY W. H. J. & J. C. WEALE

CRESCENT MOON

First published 1908. This edition © 2017.

Printed and bound in the U.S.A.
Set in Book Antiqua 10 on 14pt.
Designed by Radiance Graphics.

Thanks to the authors and publishers quoted.

British Library Cataloguing in Publication data

ISBN-13 9781861716156

CRESCENT MOON PUBLISHING
P.O. Box 1312, Maidstone, Kent, ME14 5XU
Great Britain, www.crmoon.com

CONTENTS

I.   Hans Memling   15

II.   Early Days and Training   19

III.   Earliest Works   22

IV.   Characteristics of His Early Works   26

V.   The Maturity of His Art   42

VI.   Masterpieces and Death   50

VII.   Effacement and Vindication of His Types   56

Bibliography   86

NOTE ON THE TEXT

The text is from *Memlinc* by W.H.J. Weale and J.C. Weale,
published by T.C. & E.C. Jack, London and Frederick A. Stokes,
New York, in 1901, as part of the Masterpieces In Colour series,
edited by T. Leman Hare.

The illustrations discussed in the book are included in the
illustrations section, along with many other works.

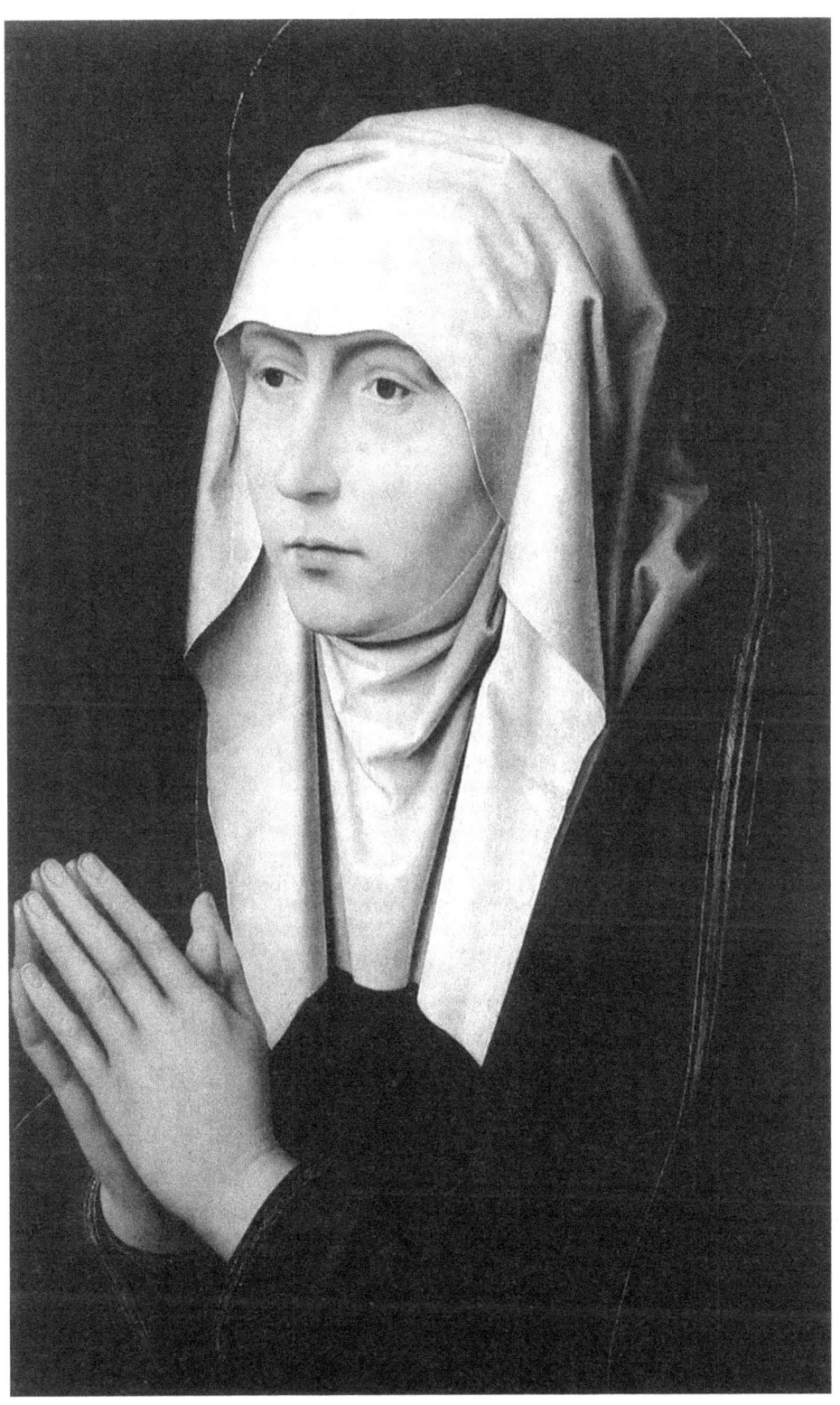

Hans Memling, Mater Dolorosa, 1480s, Uffizi Gallery

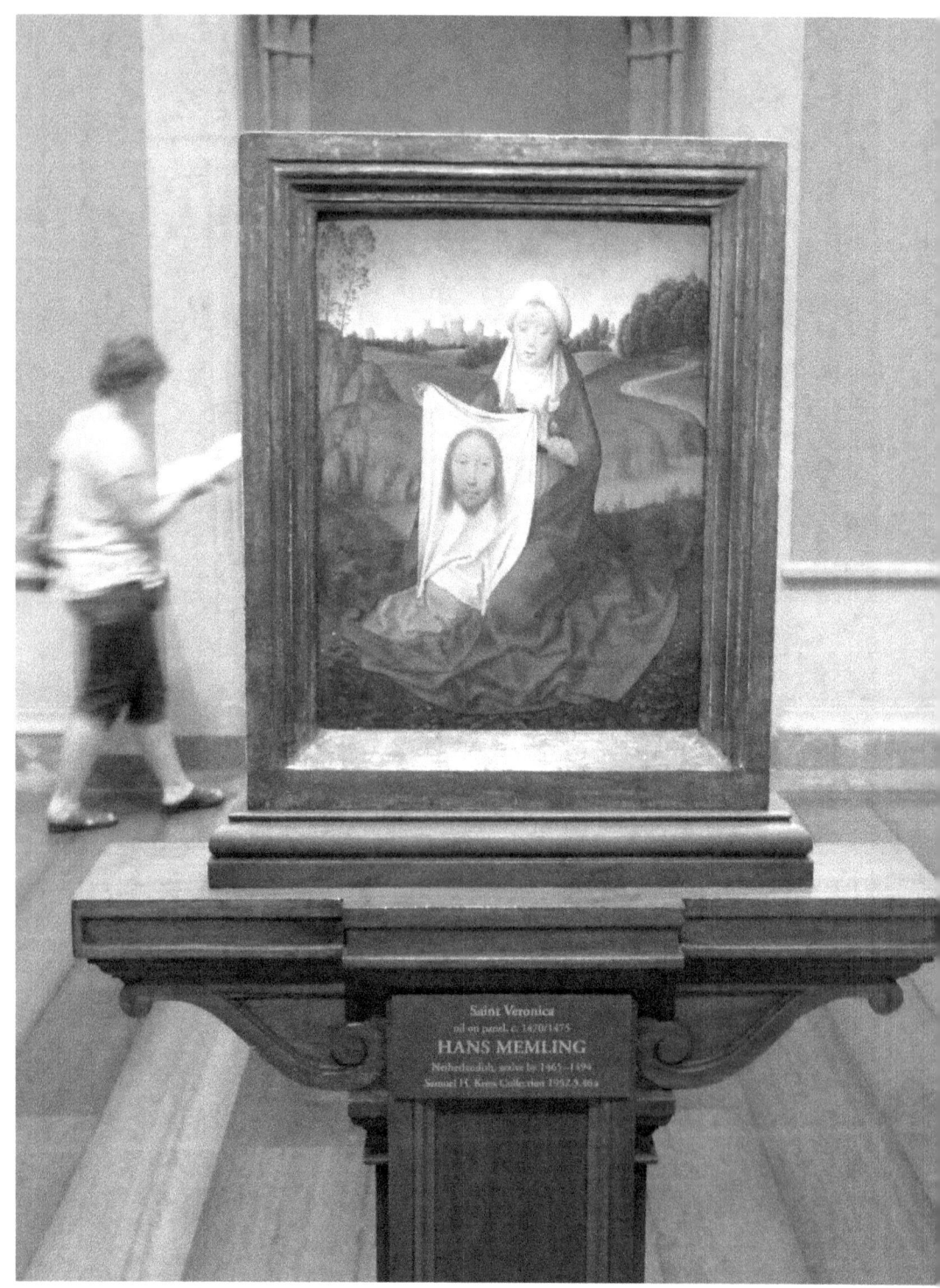

Hans Memling, St Veronica, National Gallery of Art, Washington, DC

I

HANS MEMLING

ALREADY, before the advent of the House of Burgundy, Bruges had attained the height of her prosperity. From a small military outpost of civilisation, built to stay the advance of the ravaging Northmen, she had developed through four short centuries of a strenuous existence into one of the three leading cities of northern Europe. Born to battle, fighting had been her abiding lot with but scant intervals of peace, and as it had been under the rule of her long line of Flemish counts, so it continued with increased vehemence during the century of French domination that followed, the incessant warring of suzerain and vassal being further complicated and embittered by internecine strife with the rival town of Ghent. But she emerged from the ordeal with her vitality unsapped, her industrial capabilities unabated, her commercial supremacy unshaken. Her population had reached the high total of a hundred and fifty thousand; she overlorded an outport with a further thirty thousand inhabitants, a seaport, and a number of subordinate townships. The staple of wool was established at her centre, and she was the chief emporium of the cities of the Hanseatic League. Vessels from all quarters of the globe crowded her harbours, her basins, and canals, as many as one hundred and fifty being entered inwards in the twenty-four hours. Factories of merchants from seventeen kingdoms were settled there as agents, and twenty foreign consuls had palatial residences within her walls. Her industrial life was a marvel of organisation, where fifty-four incorporated associations or guilds with a membership of many thousands found constant employment.

The artistic temperament of the people had necessarily developed on the ruder lines, in the architectural embellishment of the city, the beautifying of its squares and streets, its churches and chapels, its municipal buildings and guild halls, its markets and canal embankments. "The squares," we are told, "were adorned with fountains, its bridges with statues in bronze, the public buildings and many of the private houses with statuary and carved work, the beauty of which was heightened and brought out by polychrome and gilding; the windows were rich with storied glass, and the walls of the interiors adorned with paintings in distemper, or hung with gorgeous tapestry." But of the highest forms of Art – of literature, of music, and of painting – there was slender token. The atmosphere in which the Flemings had pursued their destinies was little calculated to develop any other than the harder and more matter-of-fact side of their nature. True, here as elsewhere, and from the earliest period of her history the great monastic institutions which dotted the country had done much for the cultivation of Art, as the remains of wood sculpture, mural paintings, and numerous illuminated manuscripts amply testify. But no great school of painting had arisen or was even possible, so true is it that the development of the artistic instincts of the community require the contemplative repose and fostering inspiration of peace. In the truest sense of the term the Flemings were not a cultured artistic race: they had certainly a high standard of taste, but their artistic sense was appreciative rather than creative – even so, a notable advance for a nation of warriors and merchants.

With the succession of the House of Burgundy to the French domination an entirely new era was ushered in. If the ambition of this new line of princes was unbounded, equally so was the success which attended its pursuit; their authority increased by leaps and bounds, and soon their court had become the wealthiest and most powerful in Europe. The high notions they entertained of their own dignity brooked no compeer in the pomp and glitter of their state. The display the guild and merchant princes and foreign representatives were capable of they should outdo: the splendour of their sovereignty should blur the brilliancy of mere civic ostentation. But while they revelled in the outward show of their supremacy, they viewed with jealous eye the great wealth and large measure of liberties enjoyed by their subjects. Their needs were great, the resources of the people commensurate; and in the alternate confiscation and resale of these liberties they found a remunerative source of revenue. But if the dukes were arrogant and unscrupulous, their subjects were no cravens, and civic shrewdness often proved more than a match for ducal craft. A fine sense of humour, however, suggested the policy of keeping these lusty burghers fully diverted the while they were not being bled or chastened: hence the constant recurrence of pacifications and triumphal entries, of regal processions and gorgeous tournaments, of public banquets and bewildering revels. It was an era of pomp and pageantry unparalleled in history, the success of which required the services of the highest talents of the day – the foremost artists to enhance its magnificence, the leading writers to chronicle its marvels.

It was Duke Philip III. who requisitioned the services of John van Eyck and showered on him bounty and patronage, and if his reign had proved as uneventful as it was the reverse, Philip's name would still survive in the reflected glory of this prince of painting. The declining days of the great duke, stricken with imbecility, certainly offered no inducement to foreign artists on the lookout for court patronage. But with his death, on the 15th of June 1467, the entire prospect was changed. Charles the Bold now succeeded to the dukedom: his solemn entry into the Flemish capital took place on Palm Sunday of the year following – an occasion marked by brilliant jousts and tournaments – and his home-coming with his bride, Margaret of York, some three months later. These events, the marriage festivities notably, called for a great array of talent, and among the leading artists engaged in planning and executing the magnificent decorations indulged in we find Peter Coustain and John Hennequart, the ducal painters; James Daret and Philip Truffin of Tournay; Francis Stoc and Livin van Lathem of Brussels; Daniel De Rycke and Hugo Van der Goes of Ghent; Govart of Antwerp; and John Du Château of Ypres. And here Hans Memling enters on the scene, already then a master-painter and accomplished artist, but of whom no previous record, of whose lifework no earlier trace, has been discovered.

II

EARLY DAYS AND TRAINING

As to where and when Memling was born, where he served his apprenticeship, and with whom he worked as a journeyman no documentary evidence has yet been discovered, and no one can confidently assert; but there exists a sufficiency of presumptive evidence to warrant certain conclusions with the help of which to construct a working biography. It appears probable that the family came from Memelynck, near Alkmaar, in north Holland, and settled at Deutichem, in Guelderland; and, on the strength of an entry copied from the diary kept by an ecclesiastical notary and clerk of the Chapter of Saint Donatian at Bruges during the years 1491 to 1498, that they subsequently removed to the ecclesiastical principality of Mainz. The subject of this monograph is likely to have been born, at some date between 1425 and 1435, either at some place within that principality, or at Deutichem previous to his parents' removal. From our knowledge of the guild system which obtained in the middle ages throughout the north of Europe with but slight variation in the conditions of training and apprenticeship, and taking into consideration besides the typical characteristics of Memling's work, it appears probable that he served his apprenticeship at Mainz, and afterwards worked at Cöln as a journeyman, and this opinion is confirmed by the outstanding fact that in all the wealth of architectural embellishment in which his pictures abound the only town outside Bruges whose buildings are faithfully reproduced is this noted centre of art. That he should have travelled thither for the especial purpose of securing an accurate background for the first, fifth, and sixth panels of the Shrine of Saint Ursula, and not have cared to obtain as faithful settings for the incidents of the second and fourth panels ascribed to Basel, or for that of the third panel located at Rome, will scarcely stand the test of criticism. A study of these panels evidences an intimate acquaintance with the architectural beauties of Cöln, a knowledge obviously acquired at first hand during a period of his life devoted to Art. The master under whom he worked was in all probability the Suabian, Stephen Löthener, of Mersburg, near Constance, who had settled in Cöln before 1442, and died there in 1452. It is presumable that Memling may not have completed his studies at the time of that painter's death. In the circumstances one can but conjecture as to where he completed the necessary training before attaining to the rank of a master-painter. Vasari and Guicciardini both assert that Memling was at some time or other a pupil of Roger De la Pasture (Van der Weyden), and, as this master returned from Italy in 1450, he may have come across Memling at Cöln and engaged him as an assistant. It is, however, quite possible that Memling stayed on at Cöln until Löthener's death in 1452 and then went to Brussels, doubtless passing by Louvain and possibly working for a time under Dirk Bouts. Certain it is, judging from the many points of similarity in their work, that Memling came under Roger's influence for a space sufficiently long to leave a strong impress of that master's methods on his art. Memling's contemporary, Rumwold De Doppere, has left it on record that he was "then considered to be the most skilful and excellent painter in the whole of Christendom"; and if Memling had left nothing to perpetuate his fame but such gems as the Shrine of Saint Ursula, at Bruges, the "Passion of Our Lord," in the Royal Museum at Turin, that remarkable altarpiece, "Christ the Light of the World," in the Royal Gallery at Munich, or even, as Fromentin suggests, only those two figures of Saint Barbara and Saint Katherine in the large altarpiece at Bruges, he would need nothing of the reflected glory of his alleged master to enhance his renown. Always assuming Memling to have stood in this relation to De la Pasture, Sir Martin Conway came to a happy conclusion when he wrote that Roger's greatest glory is that he produced such a pupil – "that Memling the artist was Roger's greatest work."

III

EARLIEST WORKS

THE first painting to bespeak his industry is now supposed to have been the famous triptych of the Last Judgment in the Church of Saint Mary at Danzig, commenced after 1465 and finished in 1472 or early in 1473.

Few pictures have evoked more controversy or been coupled with the names of more artists than the Danzig triptych. The entry in a local church register of 1616 which asserts that it was painted in Brabant by John and George van Eichen, an ascription varied at a subsequent period by substituting the name of James for John, carries no more weight than usually attaches to popular traditions, and was generally disregarded by the connoisseurs and experts who have debated the question for more than a hundred years. The names of Albert van Ouwater, Michael Wohlgemuth, Hugh Van der Goes, Hubert and John van Eyck, Roger De la Pasture, and Dirk Bouts have all been canvassed with more or less assurance. Memling's name was first associated with the work in 1843, by Hotho, whose opinion met with wide acceptance, a notable convert to his view being Dr. Waagen, who in 1860 declared the triptych to be "not only the most important work by Memling that has come down to our time, but also one of the masterpieces of the whole school, being far richer and better composed than the picture of the same subject by Roger De la Pasture at Beaune, though that master's influence is still perceptible," though two years later he recognised in the figures the influence of Dirk Bouts; and in 1899 Kämmerer as emphatically declared that "no one who is acquainted with Memling's authentic works can possibly doubt that this picture is the work of his hand." In the absence of contemporary documentary evidence, and with the donors of the picture still unidentified, confronted moreover with the fact that in its composition the Danzig triptych differs altogether from Memling's authenticated paintings, many experienced judges still hesitated to admit the claim put forward in his behalf. But the recent discoveries made by Dr. A. Warburg leave little room for doubt. In the fifteenth century there was a considerable Italian colony at Bruges, and the powerful Florentine firm of the Medici, whose ramifications extended over all Europe, had a branch establishment there in the name of Piero and Giovanni de' Medici, the acting manager of which from 1455 to 1466 was Angelo di Jacopo Tani, who, after serving as bookkeeper of the firm's agency in London, had been transferred to Bruges in 1450. Tani may have taken Memling into his household with a view to the production of the triptych under his own eye. The absence of Memling's name from the guild registers of the period lends probability to the theory that he was employed by Charles the Bold, for ducal service exempted painters settling in Bruges from the obligation of purchasing the right of citizenship, and of becoming members of the local guild. It is presumed that Tani engaged Memling's services at some date after 1465 to paint or, if the work had been commenced by some other painter, to complete this picture. While the dexter shutter, representing the reception of the elect by Saint Peter at the gate of Heaven, can only have been designed by a pupil of Löthener, it is equally certain that the upper portion of the central panel must have been designed by some one who had worked under Bouts or De la Pasture. In 1466 Tani visited Florence, and there married

Katherine, daughter of William Tanagli. As their portraits and arms are on the exterior of the shutters, these cannot have been commenced before they were both in Bruges, some time in 1467, the date inscribed on the slab covering a tomb on which a woman is seated. The technique and colouring of the entire work are Netherlandish, and in the opinion of the most trustworthy critics are certainly the work of Memling. The painting completed, it was, at the commencement of 1473, despatched by sea to Florence, but the vessel bearing it was captured by freebooters, and the picture as part of the prize carried off to Danzig.

The patronage of the agent of the Medici was of course of incalculable advantage to a rising artist, and doubtless it served to secure for Memling the interest of Spinelli of Arezzo – whose portrait, now in the van Ertborn collection at the Antwerp Museum, he painted in the latter half of 1467 or the beginning of 1468, when this Italian medallist was in the service of Charles the Bold as seal engraver – and to bring his growing reputation to the notice of the ducal court. The negotiations for the hand of Margaret of York, begun in December 1466, and unduly protracted owing no doubt to the mental incapacity of Duke Philip III., were of course resumed at the expiration of the period of court mourning after his death on 15th June 1467. Following the example of his father, Charles may have commissioned Memling to accompany his ambassadors to the English court for the purpose of securing an up-to-date portrait of his intended consort. In the circumstances Memling would certainly have made the acquaintance of Sir John Donne, for the Donnes were ardent Yorkists high in the royal favour, and moreover the brother of Sir John's wife, William, first Lord Hastings, filled the office of Lord Chamberlain to the king. But the triptych in the Chatsworth collection, though the outcome of this meeting, could not have been executed at the time, as the period of Memling's visit would have been restricted to carrying out the ducal instructions. An opportunity for the necessary sittings was afforded later, when Sir John Donne, accompanied by his wife and daughter, journeyed to

Bruges in the suite of the princess to assist at the wedding celebrations in July 1468. The omission of the sons from the family group in the triptych is sufficiently accounted for by the fact that they were in Wales at the time.

IV

CHARACTERISTICS OF
HIS EARLY WORKS

TO the art student these earliest of Memling's paintings – the Donne triptych in particular – are replete with interest. In the first place, they attest the powers then already at the painter's command as an exponent of his art, and they further serve as a standard of comparison by which to judge his afterwork. Memling was pre-eminently a religious artist, deeply imbued with Scriptural lore and well versed in hagiography, a fund of knowledge sublimated in the beautiful mysticism of the school of Cöln which had early subjugated his poetic temperament. His conception of the Madonna, based on a fervent appreciation of the purity, the tenderness, and the majesty of her nature was deeply rooted, and it led him to evolve the definite type which he presents to us in the Chatsworth picture, to which he faithfully adheres henceforth, at times enhancing its beauty – as witness the triptych in the Louvre and the altarpiece of Saint John's Hospital at Bruges – until his ideal culminates in that marvellous embodiment of her supreme attributes preserved to us in the Van Nieuwenhove diptych. The Divine Infant, it is true, may not appeal to one in the same way as do the charming pictures of infant life in which the southern artists excelled. Whatever may be said of the fine men and intellectual women of the race, the northern type of babyhood cannot by any stretch of courtesy, apart from a mother's loving weakness, be described as graceful. Still Memling's conceptions of the Infant Saviour rank high in point of intellectuality, of expressiveness of eye, of grace of movement and charm of expression. The Donne triptych besides, from the point of view from which we are now considering it, is a valuable asset for the study of the impersonations of saints whom we find constantly recurring in his paintings: to wit, Saint Katherine and Saint Barbara – (Fromentin's enthusiastic appreciation of these figures in the large altarpiece at Bruges has already been quoted) – Saint John the Baptist and Saint John the Evangelist, and Saint Christopher. The same may be said of his angels. Taken from another standpoint, these early paintings of Memling are invaluable testimony of his rare gift for portraiture. It was a gift which may almost be taken as the specific appanage of the fifteenth century painters of the Netherlandish school. Some, like John van Eyck, used it with scrupulous exactitude, scorning to veil the palpable truth that at the moment and usually obtruded itself on his painstaking eye; others, and Memling prominently of their number, loved rather to seize on the fitful manifestation of the inner man and to idealise him. Both artists, taking them as types, were honest and true to their art, notwithstanding that the resulting truth in each case is deceiving, except we have very particular information regarding the individual portrayed. In any event, the Tani and Spinelli portraits are fine examples of the class, though perhaps Sir John Donne's appeals to us more because of the fuller knowledge we have of the man. And finally, both the Antwerp and the Chatsworth paintings afford us beautiful examples of Memling's art as a landscape painter, and in this respect certainly it may be safely asserted that he never produced better work.

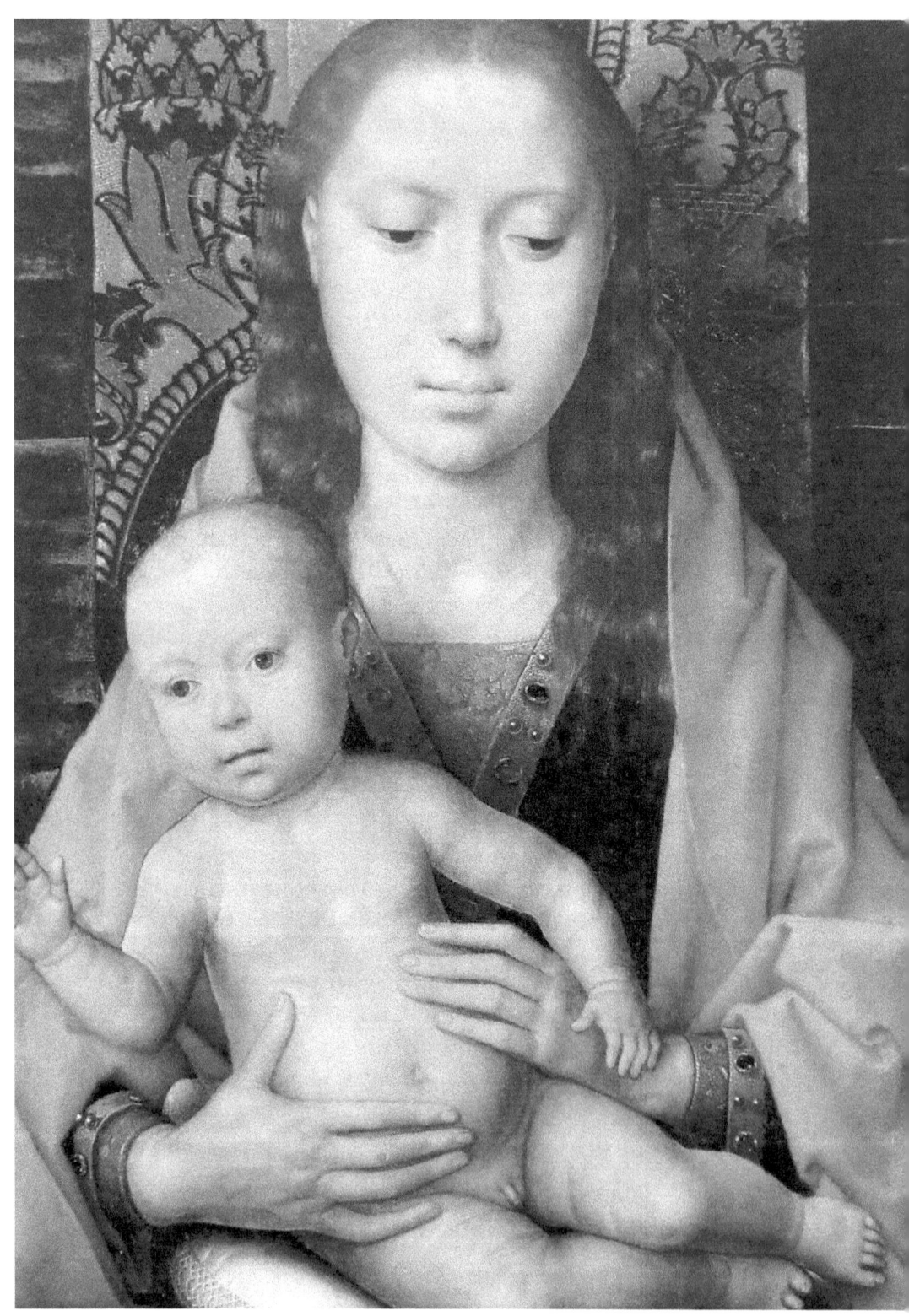

Hans Memling, Madonna and Child, National Gallery, London

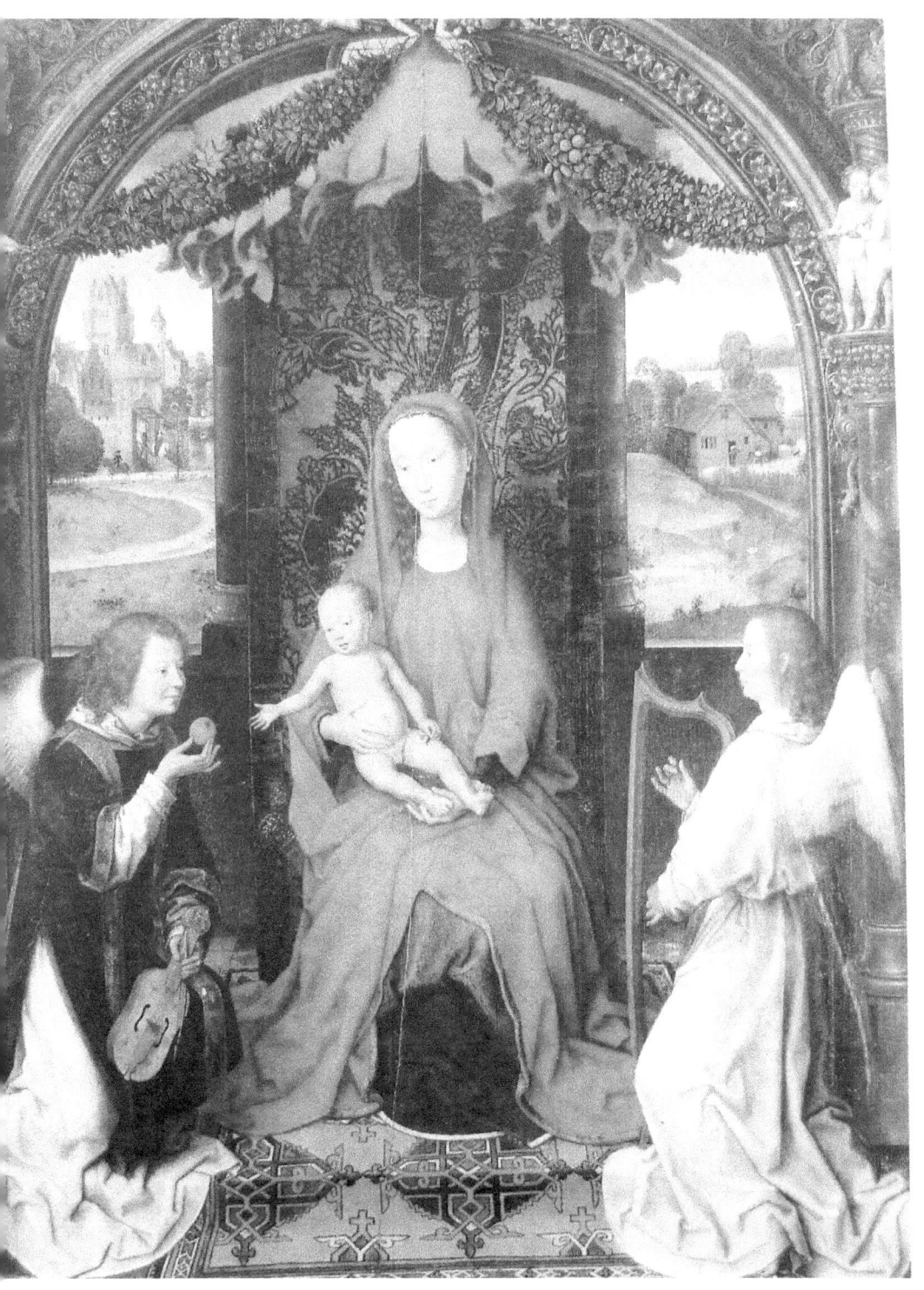

Hans Memling, Virgin and Child Enthroned, Vienna

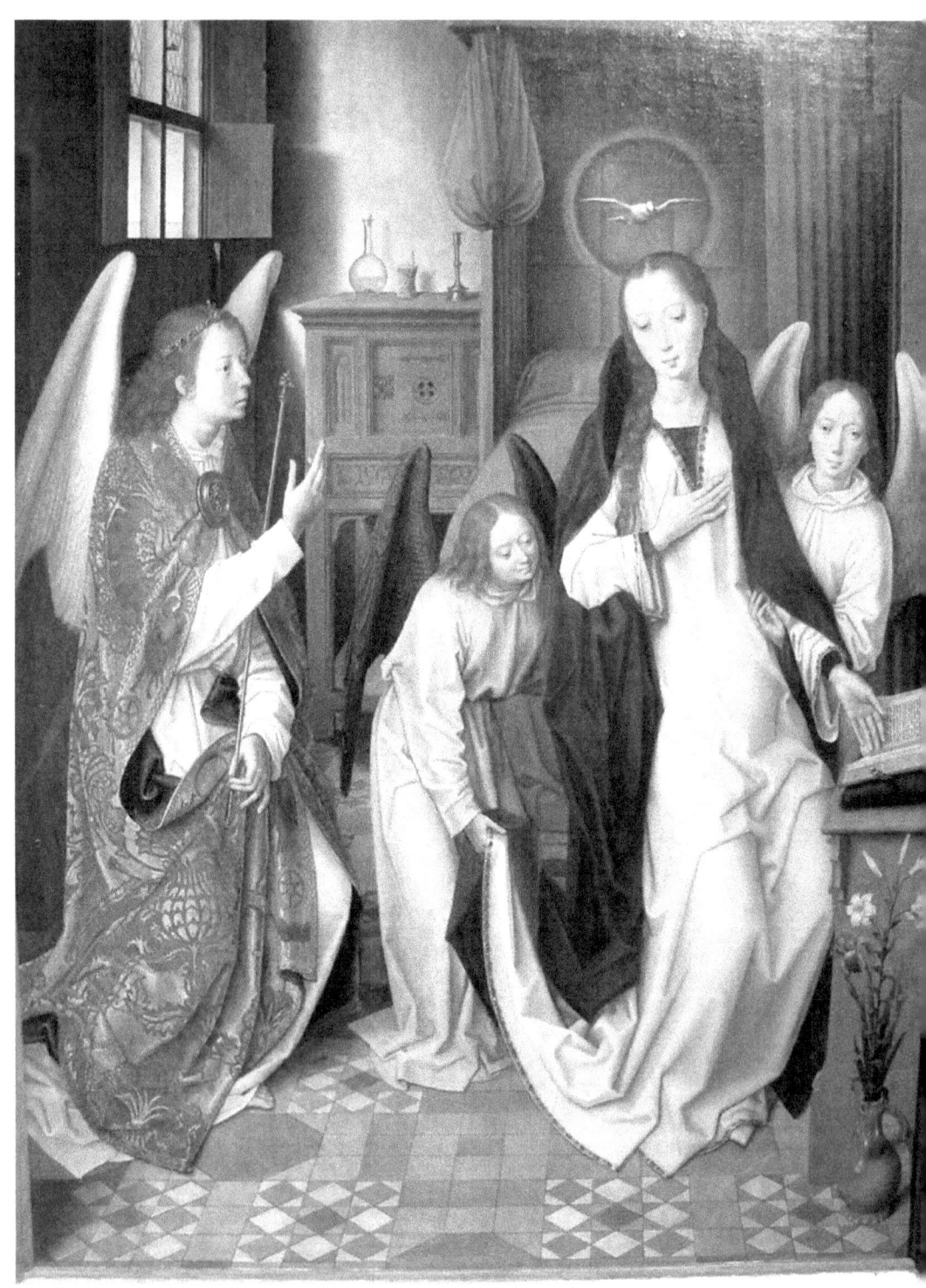

Hans Memling, The Annunciation, 1480-89,
Metropolitan Museum of Art, New York City

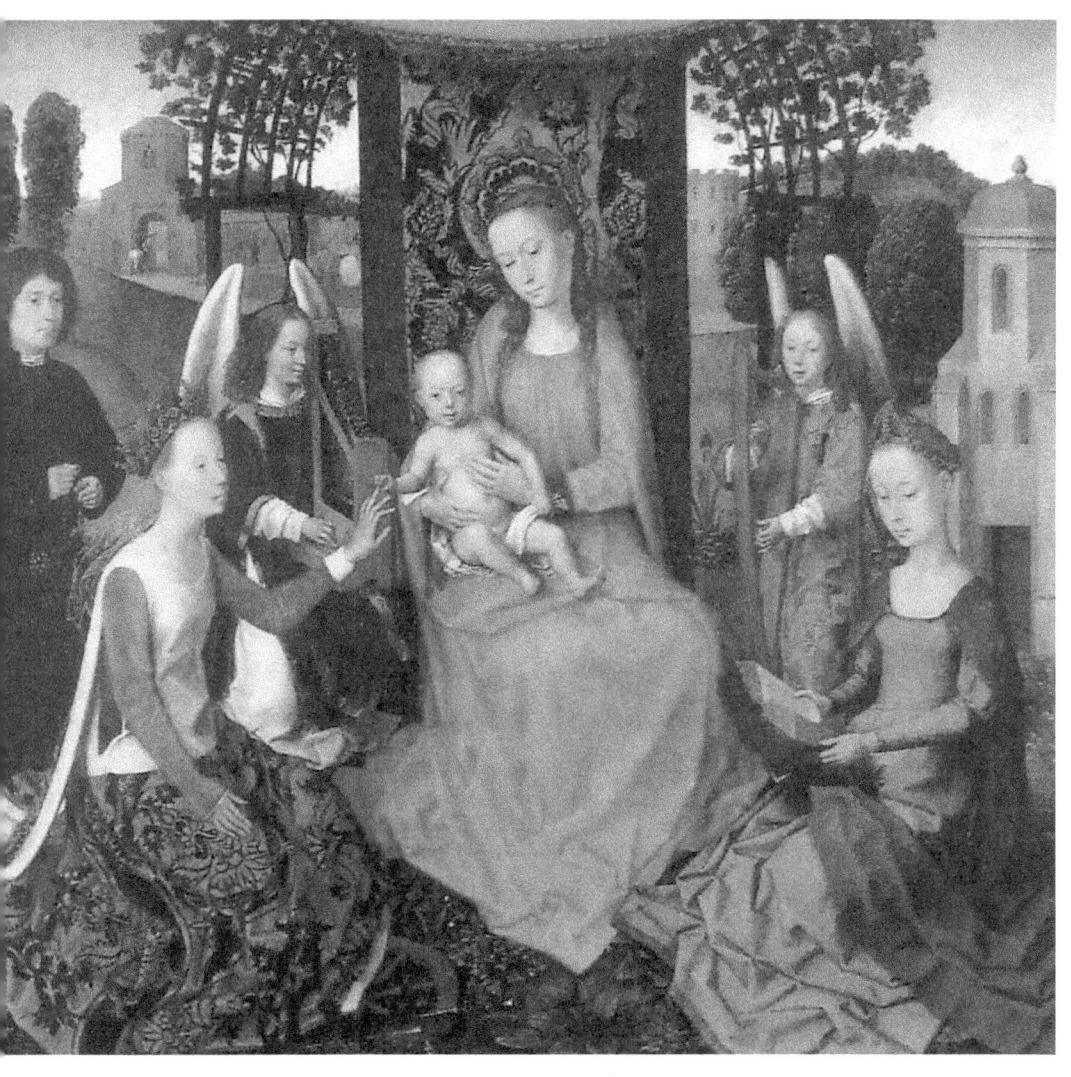

Hans Memling, The Mystic Marriage of St Catherine, Metropolitan
Museum, New York City

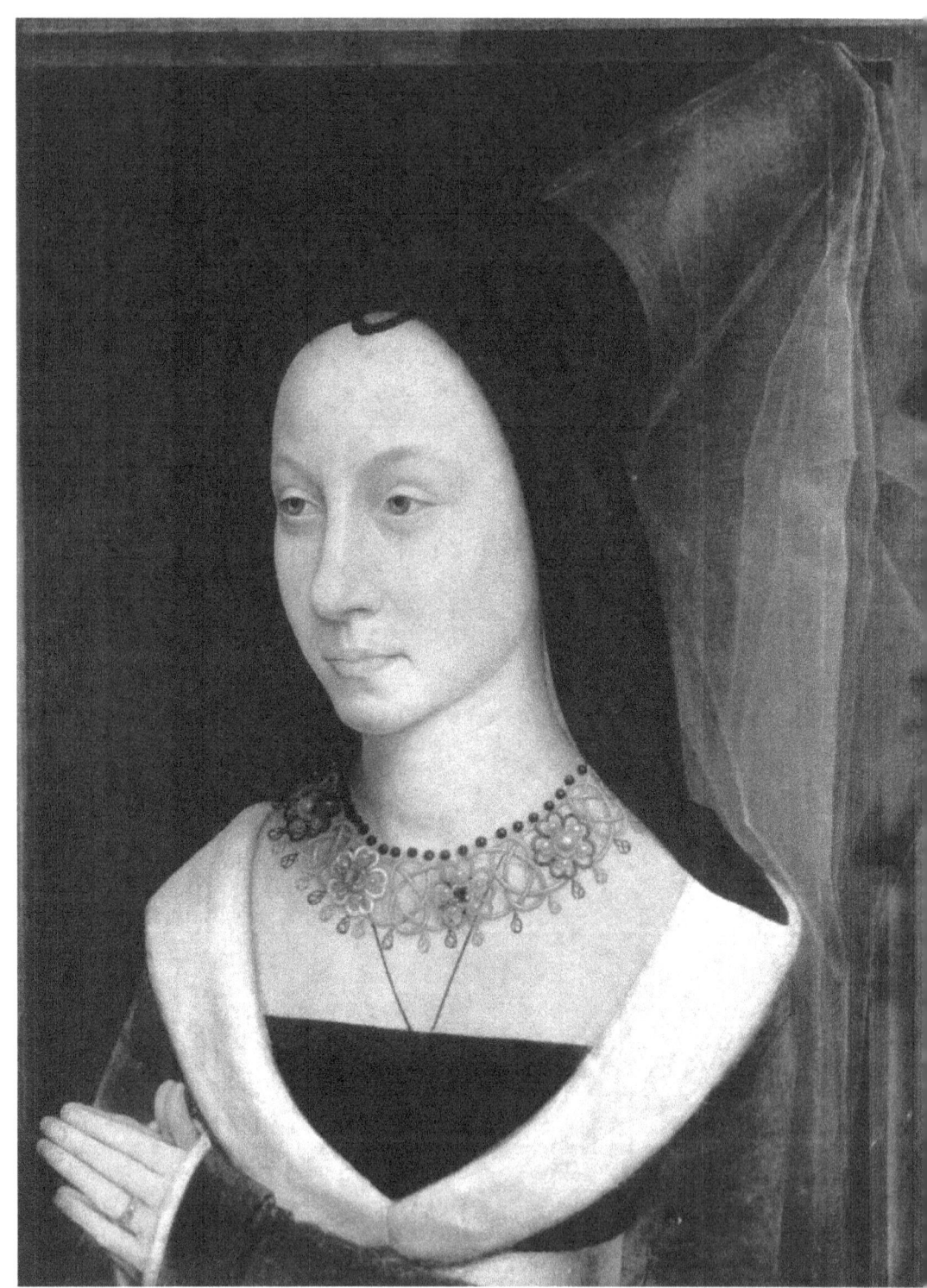

Hans Memling, Portrait of Maria Portinari, 1470s,
Metropolitan Museum of Art, New York City

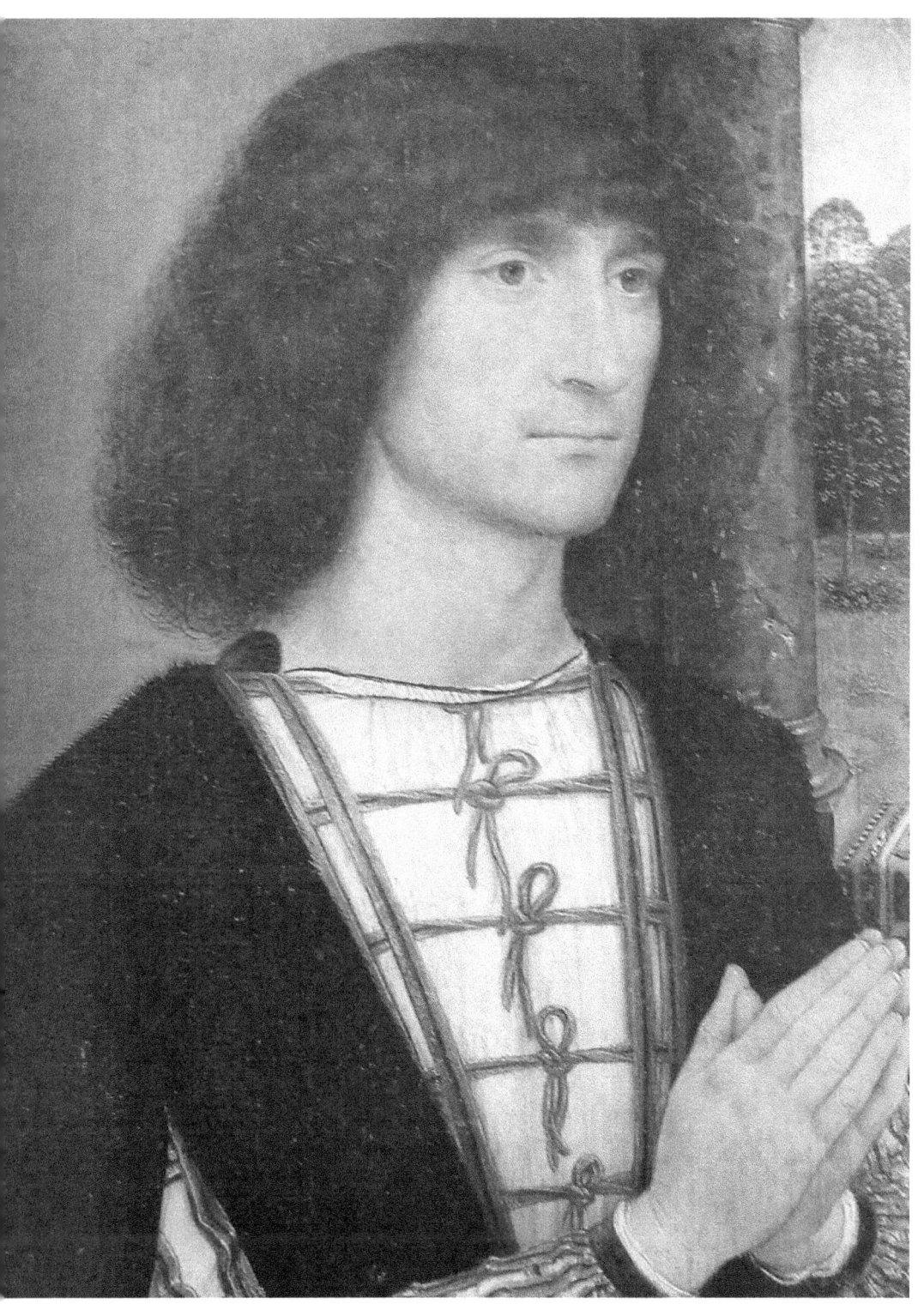

Hans Memling, Young Man At Prayer, 1485, Thyssen Collection

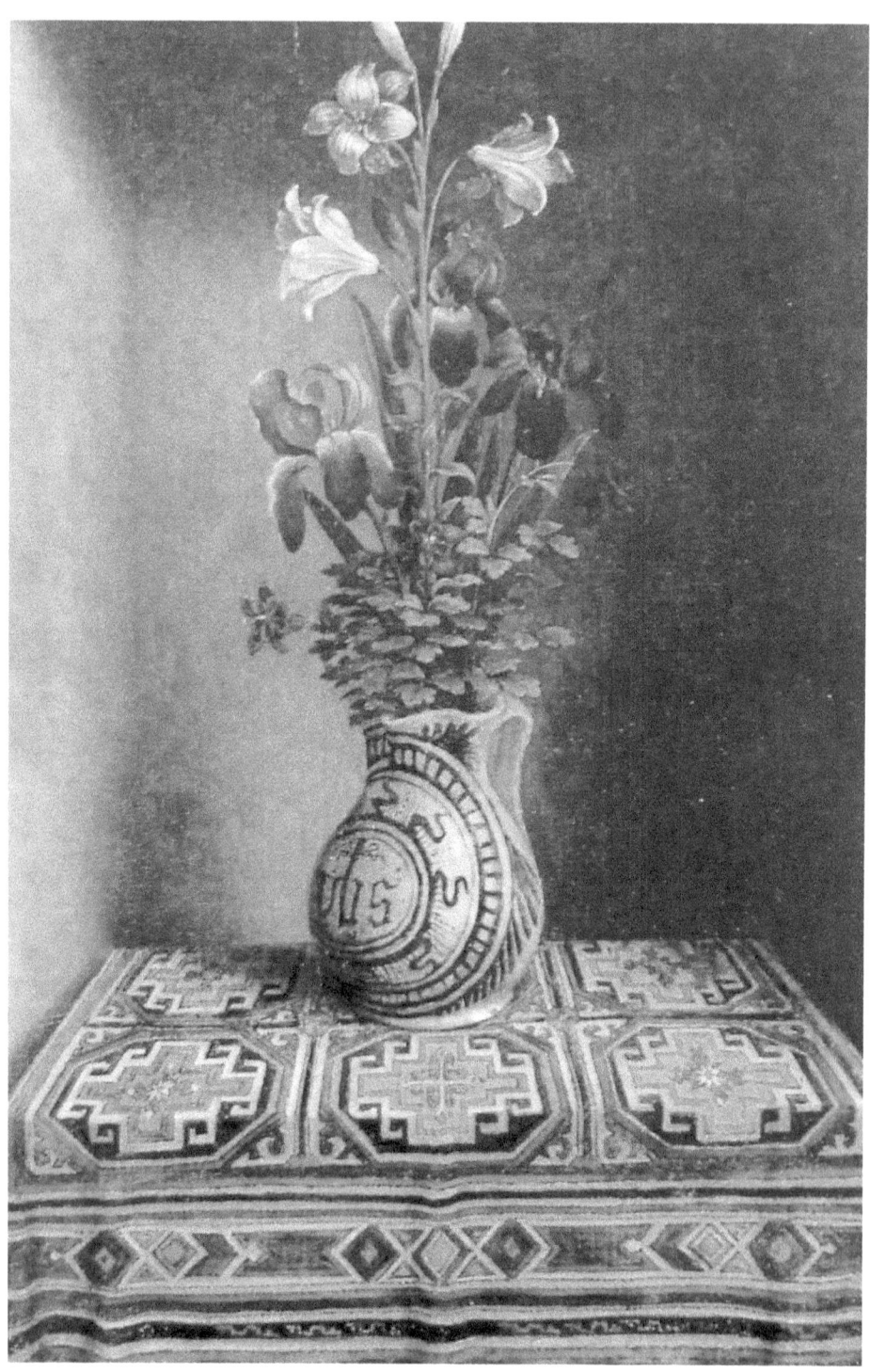

Hans Memling, Marian Flowerpiece, 1485,
Thyssen-Bornemisza Collection

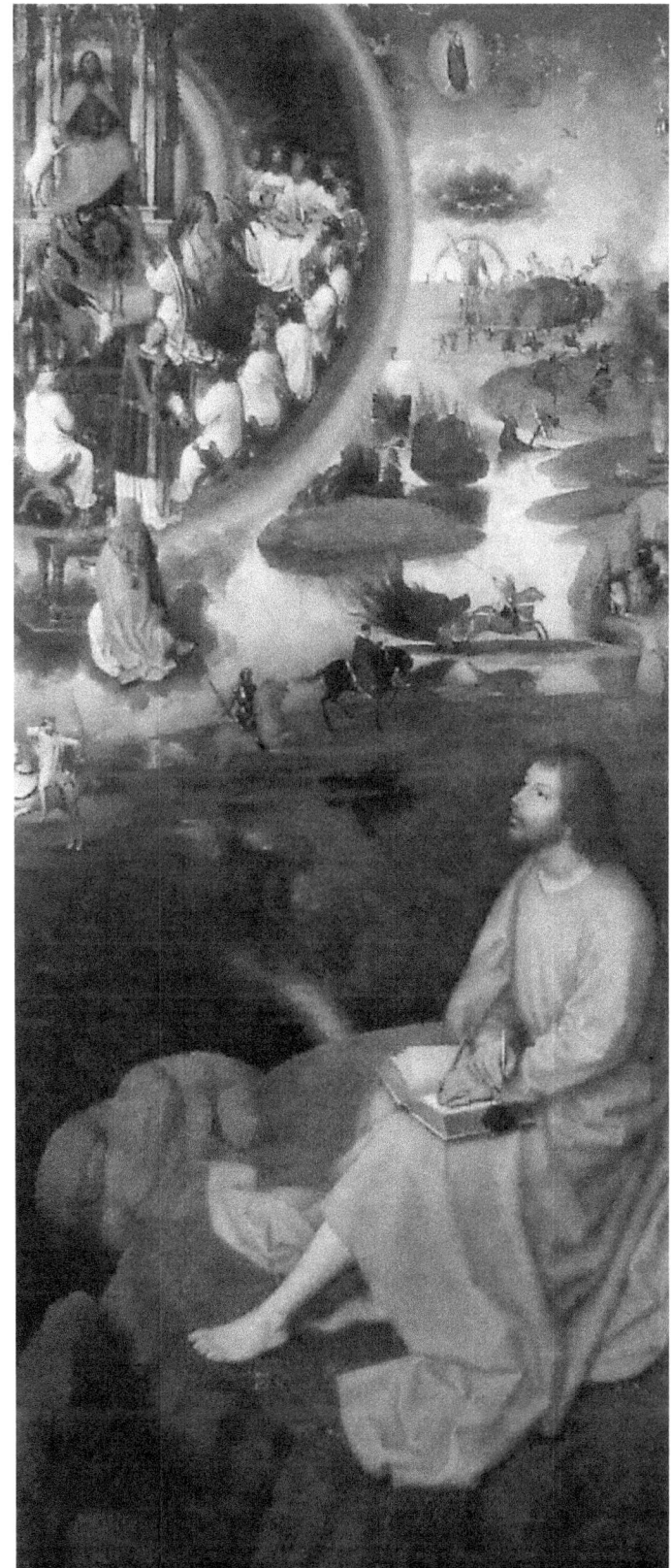

Hans Memling,
John On Patmos,
Bruges

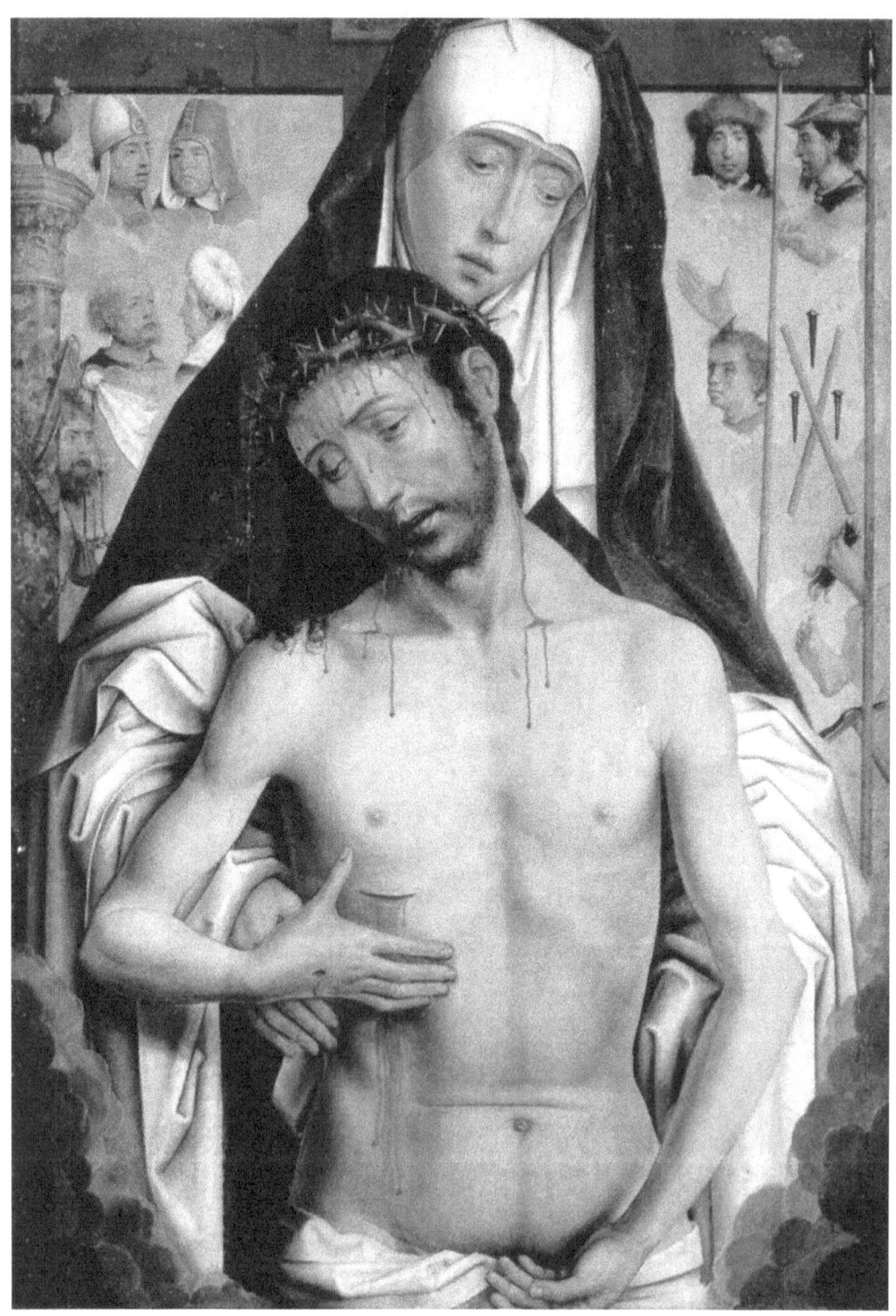

Hans Memling, Pietà, 1480, Granada

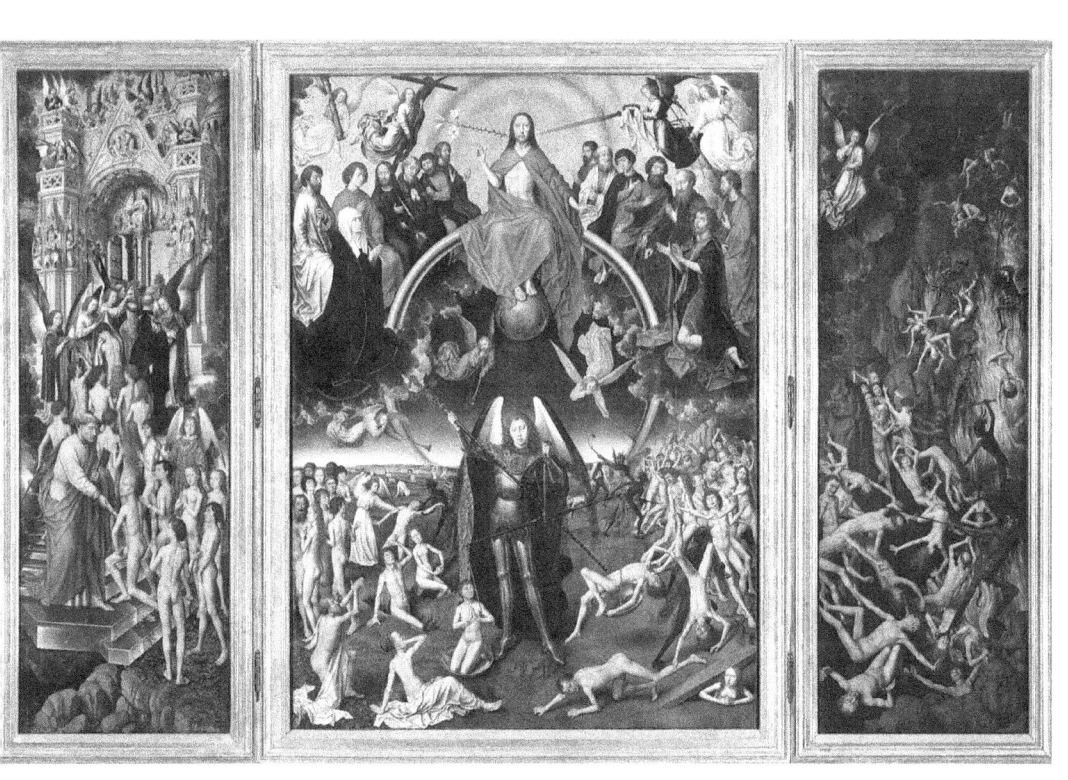

Hans Memling, The Last Judgement, Gdansk

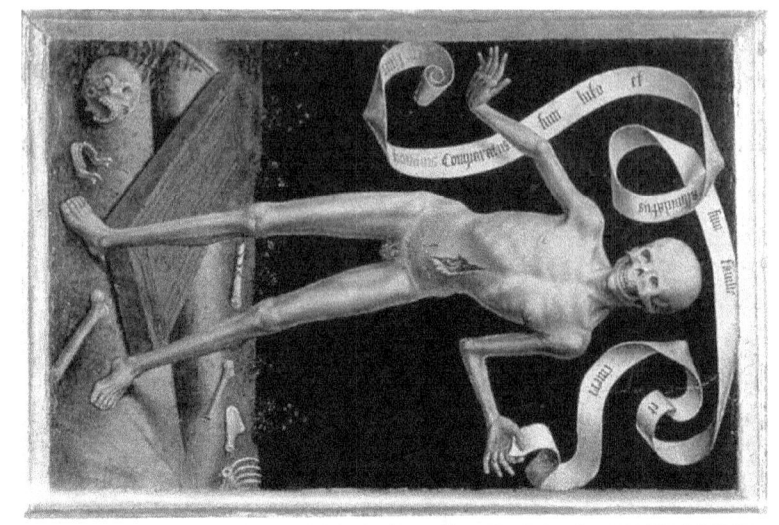

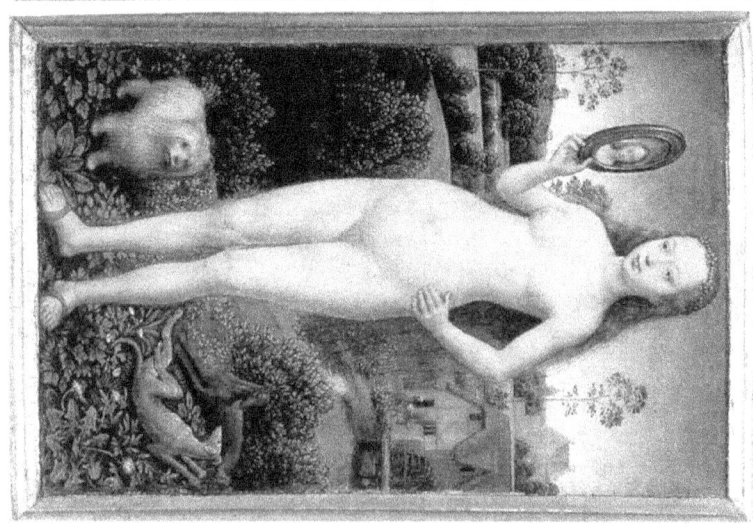

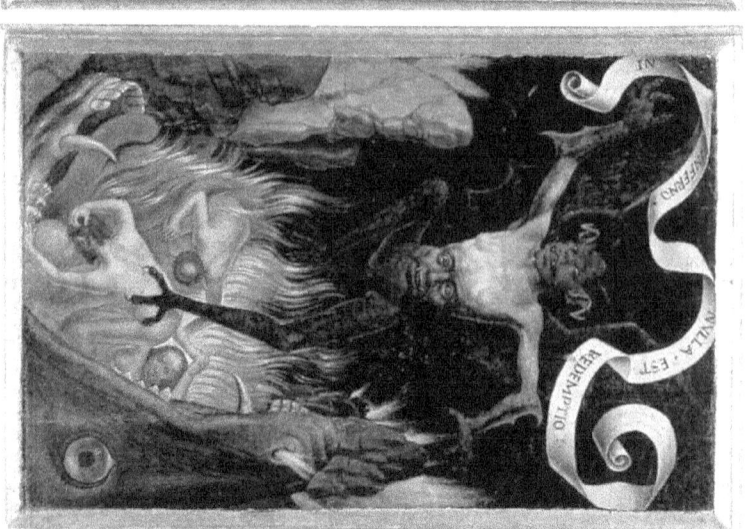

Hans Memling, Triptych of Earthly Vanity and Divine Salvation, 1485, Strasbourg

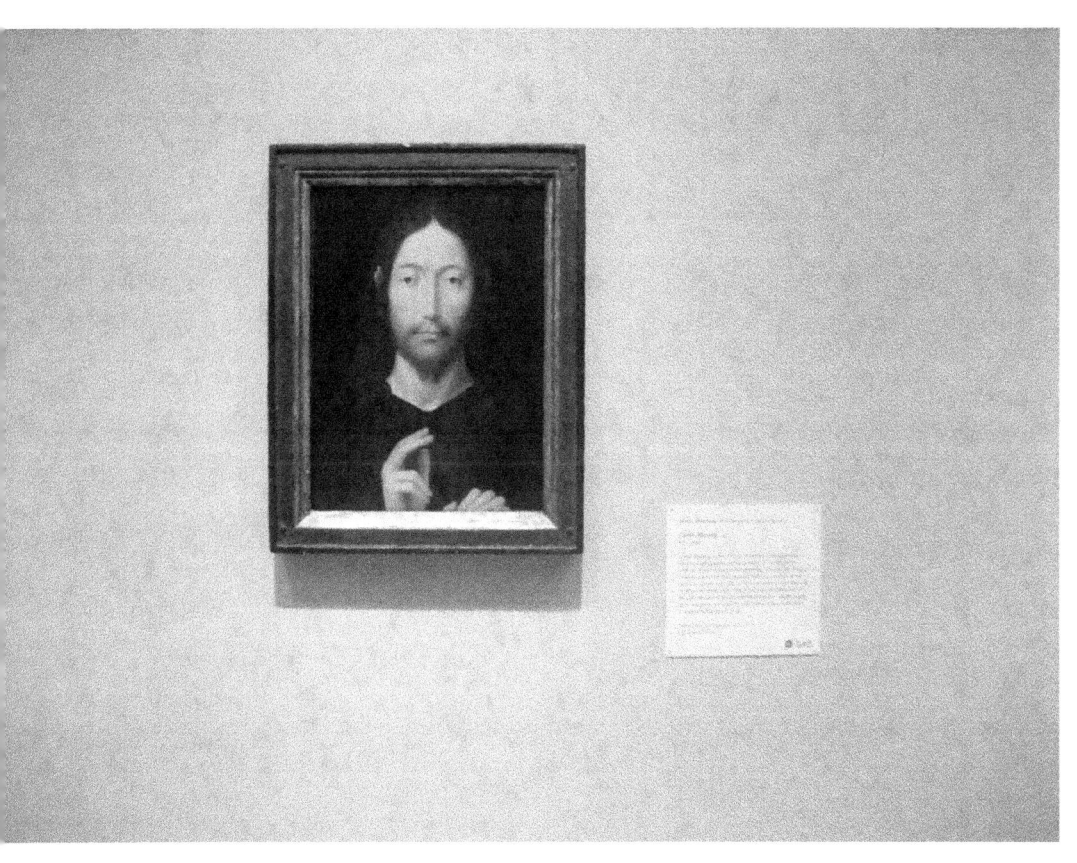

Hans Memling, Christ Blessing, Metropolitan Museum of Art

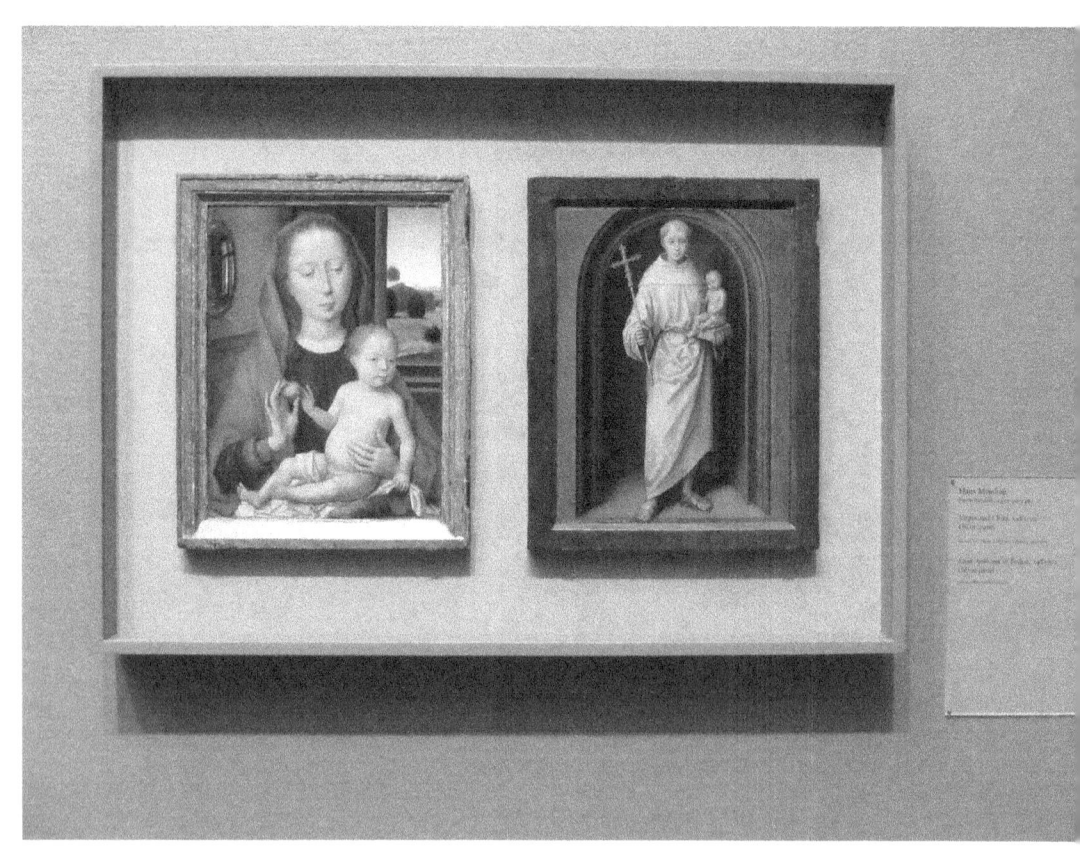

Hans Memling, Madonna and Child, Metropolitan Museum of Art, Gotham

V

THE MATURITY OF HIS ART

FROM the consideration of these three works executed in the sixties we pass on to a decade of more notable achievement. The public rejoicings which had inaugurated the new reign were already dimmed to recollection in the disquieting civil and national complications that ensued, culminating in the disastrous battle of Nancy on 5th January 1477, in which the ducal troops were put to rout and Charles himself lost his life. He was succeeded by his only daughter, Mary, who on 19th August of the same year by her marriage to Maximilian, son of the Emperor Frederick IV., brought Flanders under the rule of the House of Austria, and thus involved the Flemish burghers in that lamentable struggle which, after many alternations of fortune, was one of the chief causes that led to the downfall of Bruges. Memling, as a newcomer without rooted interests or strong political bent, wholly wrapt in his art, naturally steered clear of political entanglements, though ready enough on occasion to take his share of the public burden which the fortune of war imposed, as witness his contribution to the loan raised to cover the expenses of the military operations against France. But his placid disposition shrank from the heat and ferment of public life, though his sympathies no doubt were all with the burghers and guildmen with whom he associated, among whom he found the most liberal supporters of his art to the exclusion of court patronage, and from whose womankind he selected a helpmate. Memling married later in life than was the custom of his day, when it was usual for craftsmen to take unto themselves a wife at the expiration of their journeymanship, after they had established their competence, paid the indispensable guild fees, and taken the no less essential vows to bear themselves honestly and to labour their work as in the sight of God; for it was only at some date between 1470 and 1480, when already a man of middle age, that he led Anne, daughter of Louis De Valkenaere, to the altar. It is impossible to determine the year, but on the 10th of December 1495 we find the guardians of the three children of the marriage acting on their behalf in the local courts in the winding-up of their father's estate, which at any rate proves that the eldest at that time must have been still a minor, or under the age of five-and-twenty. Apart from his wife's dowry, of which we have no knowledge, Memling's circumstances were then already much above the ordinary, for in 1480 out of the 247 wealthiest citizens only 140 were taxed at higher rates, and it is on record that in the same year he purchased a large stone house and two smaller adjacent ones on the east side of the main street that leads from the Flemish Bridge to the ramparts, in a quarter of the town much affected by artists, and within the Parish of Saint Giles, beneath the spreading trees of whose peaceful God's acre he was to find an abiding resting-place some fourteen years later, by the side of his old friend the miniaturist William Vrelant, who predeceased him by some thirteen years, to be joined there in after years by many another eminent artist, such as John Prévost, Lancelot Blondeel, Peter Pourbus, and Antony Claeissens.

That he was a busy man the record of works that have come down to us from this decade alone amply testifies. The "Saint John the Baptist," in the Royal Gallery at Munich (1470); the exquisite little diptych "The Blessed Virgin and Child," in the Louvre, painted (*c.* 1475) for John Du Celier, a member of the Guild of Merchant Grocers, whose father was a member of the Council of Flanders; the panel in the National Gallery, which we reproduce; the magnificent altarpiece in the Royal Museum at Turin painted for William Vrelant (1478); the famous triptych executed for the high altar of the church attached to the Hospital of Saint John at Bruges (1479); and the triptych "The Adoration of the Magi" presented to the Hospital by Brother John Floreins (1479), all belong to this period: while with the year 1480 are associated the portraits of William Moreel and his wife, in the Royal Gallery at Brussels; that of one of their daughters as the Sibyl Sambetha, in Saint John's Hospital; the marvellous composition in the Royal Gallery at Munich, "Christ the Light of the World," painted to the order of Peter Bultinc, a wealthy citizen of Bruges and a member of the Guild of Tanners; and the triptych "The Dead Christ mourned by His Mother," in Saint John's Hospital – let alone the numerous other works attributed to him but not authenticated or which have been lost. The bare record, however, conveys but a feeble idea of the immensity of the labour this output involved.

The panel in the National Gallery, which may be ascribed to 1475, arrests our attention for the moment. It presents to us the Blessed Virgin and Child in attitudes closely corresponding to those in the earlier Donne triptych, but both are more pleasing figures in respect of pose, the attitude of the Madonna in particular being less constrained and the expression happier and more natural. The figure of the angel too has gained in gracefulness. The donor under the patronage of Saint George appeals to one as a living personality. Of these two figures a lady critic complains that they are "characteristic examples of Memling's inability to depict a really manly man"; and she endeavours to give greater point to this criticism by contrasting the painter's methods with those of John van Eyck, wholly of course to the disadvantage of the former. In the present case the identity of the donor remains a mystery: he may not have been the really manly man the idealist would require, and also he may have been the man of reverent and sweet disposition revealed to us in this portrait. It is for the softening and idealisation of the face from the reality, however, that fault is commonly found with Memling as a portrait-painter. But, after all, what is this idealisation of the subject but the highest aim and truest concept of art? It is no difficult matter for the competent painter to produce a counterpart of the outward flesh with all its peculiarities, even to the last wrinkle and the least significant blemish, and be awarded the palm for "stern realism"; but to conceive the inner soul of the man, to seize and fix that conception on panel or canvas, surely that is the higher art? It is true that in the men whom Memling portrayed there is a marked similarity of expression, arising obviously from the fact that they are usually pictured in an attitude of devotion, and that in the frame of mind this attitude imposed they suffered some loss of workaday individuality. But surely it is not to Memling's discredit that his clients were of the devotional order? Nor is the criticism of the Saint George as mild and effeminate any more to the point; for when the appeal is from Memling to Van Eyck one is forcibly reminded of the votive picture of the Virgin and Child by that master in the Town Gallery at Bruges, in which we have the donor under the patronage of a Saint George whom for sheer inanity of expression and utter awkwardness of demeanour it would be hard to beat. And yet in neither instance, we may safely assume, was the figure the type the artist would have created for the valiant knight of the legend. Apart from this, a careful study of Memling's many works will reveal to the most exacting a sufficiency of evidence that his art was equal to any demands that might have been made of it; of his preference for the milder and more religious type of man, however, there can be no doubt.

It were idle to speculate as to the length of time Memling devoted to the production of his pictures, seeing the meagreness of the data afforded us for the purpose. His peculiar technique, however, which avoided the accentuation of light and shade, and thereby simplified the scheme of colouring, lent itself to rapid execution. Even so, paintings like the altarpiece in the Royal Museum at Turin and that in the Royal Gallery at Munich must have made heavy calls on his time through a number of years. As examples of the powers and wealth of resource of the artist these masterpieces stand almost alone. The architectural setting of the former, a wholly imaginary Jerusalem, is so contrived as to assist in the most natural manner the precession of the Gospel story from the triumphal entry into the Holy City to the Resurrection and the manifestation of Christ to Mary Magdalene. As without conscious effort the eye is guided along the line of route followed by the Redeemer, one treads in imagination in the Divine footsteps through the hosannahing multitude in the extreme background on the right, and turning to the left arrives at the Temple steps in time to witness the casting out of the buyers and sellers; descending thence and bearing gradually towards the right a turn of the street leads one to the scene of the Last Supper, which Judas has already left to confer with the priests under a neighbouring portico as to the betrayal of his Master; and eventually one arrives at the Garden of Olives, to be confronted in rapid succession with the Agony and the picture of the sleeping disciples, the rush of armed men, Judas' traitorous kiss and Peter in the act of striking at Malchus. Following the multitude for some little distance one reaches the heart of the city, where the successive incidents of the Passion are grouped each under a separate portico showing on to a spacious courtyard in the very centre of the panel – Christ before Pilate and his expostulating wife, the Flagellation, the Crowning with thorns and mocking of Our Lord, Christ before Herod and the Ecce Homo, with the preparations for the Crucifixion going on the while in the open courtyard. These completed, the mournful procession passes under a palace gateway into the forefront of the picture, bears to the left and issues through the city gate, where the Mother of Christ, the beloved disciple, and the holy women have gathered together, into the open country, where at the foot of the hilly way that skirts the city walls Simon of Cyrene comes forward to relieve the fallen Saviour in the burden of the Cross; presently the procession is lost to view at a bend of the road only to reappear on the slopes of Calvary, which is triplicated here for the purpose of re-enacting the three scenes associated with it – of the Nailing to the Cross, of the Death of Our Lord, and of the Descent from the Cross. Lower down on the left we assist at the Entombment and at the Deliverance of the Just from Limbo, and further away we witness the Resurrection and, in the far background, the manifestation of Our Lord to Mary Magdalene. Viewed as a whole it is a marvel of composition enhanced by a brilliancy of colouring, and every scene in it a delicately finished miniature. Apart from the architectural setting, the three Calvaries, and the duplication of the Holy Sepulchre imposed by the necessity of representing both the Entombment and the Resurrection, the most captious can discover nothing to abate the enthusiastic admiration which this altarpiece excites, or one's wonder at the masterful manner in which Memling has succeeded in developing the story of the Passion in some twenty scenes necessitating the introduction of considerably over two hundred figures, apart from the animal and bird life that supplements them, within the narrow compass of a panel only fifty-five centimetres high by ninety centimetres in breadth! The extreme corners of the foreground are filled in with exquisite portraits of the donors, the miniaturist William Vrelant and his wife, for whom one feels that Memling has tried to excel himself in this masterwork.

Scarcely less surprising as a composition is the story in bright luminous colours told in the Munich altarpiece, a work of considerably larger dimensions (80 by 180 centimetres), commonly described as "The Seven Joys of Mary," but for which the more appropriate title has been suggested of "Christ the Light of the World." It is the story of the manifestation of Our Lord to the Gentile world in the persons of the Wise Men from the East, closely correspondent, as was Memling's wont, to the Gospel narrative and Christian tradition, except perhaps in this one respect, that the artist's innate love of moving water has suggested to him the original conceit of depicting the departing Magi as setting sail for their distant homes across the boundless waters. This portion of the background and the greater wealth of surrounding landscape greatly relieves the architectural setting, which is not so overpowering as in the Turin altarpiece. The composition too, as becomes the subject, is teeming with the joy of life in varying aspects. Here we have the gay cavalcade with streaming banners galloping along the road to Bethlehem, there the shepherds peacefully tending their flocks on the grassy slope, their watch beguiled by the strains of a bagpipe; here the scene at the Manger, all love and devotion, and the running stream nigh by at which the horses are being watered the while the Magi are making their act of adoration, there the kings with their retinues triumphantly riding away over the rocky heights; anon we have the sequence of miracles that attended the Flight of the Holy Family into Egypt – the wheat that grew and ripened in a day, the date-palm bending to offer its fruit to the Virgin Mother resting beneath its shade while the unsaddled ass grazes as it lists and Joseph fetches water from a neighbouring spring; elsewhere the risen Christ appearing to the fishing apostles, and far beyond across the waters in the background the setting of the sun in all its glory. Every scene that lends itself to the treatment has its beauty enhanced by the beauties of Nature. The one sorrowful incident in the whole story, the Massacre of the Innocents, is a mere suggestion of this cruel episode. Memling's nature shrank from the interpretation of evil, and in this particular instance has admirably succeeded in commemorating the incident of the massacre without involving it in any of its horror. A pleasing innovation may also be noticed in the treatment of his portraits of donors, Peter Bultinc and his son being introduced as devout spectators of the scene presented in the stable at Bethlehem, which they humbly contemplate through an opening in the wall. "The more one examines this picture, the greater one's astonishment at the amount of work which Memling has lavished on it, at the exquisite beauty of the various scenes, the marvellous ingenuity displayed in separating them one from another, and the skill with which they balance and are brought into one harmonious whole."

The Turin altarpiece was completed not later than 1478, in which year William Vrelant gave it to the Guild of Saint Luke and Saint John (Stationers); the Munich one at any rate some time before Easter 1480, at which date the donor presented it to the Guild of Tanners. But already then Memling had undertaken the triptych in the Hospital of Saint John painted to the order of its spiritual master, Brother John Floreins, acknowledged to be technically the most perfect work he completed before the end of 1480; and also the larger triptych for the high altar of the Hospital church.

VI

MASTERPIECES AND DEATH

MEANWHILE the contest in which the burghers of Bruges had become involved through the disputes between the States of Flanders and Maximilian over the guardianship of his son, was precipitating the decay of the town which the relentless forces of Nature had long since decreed. As early as 1410 the navigation of the great haven of the Zwijn had become impeded, and so rapidly had the silting up advanced that before the close of the century no vessel of any considerable draught was able to enter the port of Damme. Entirely engrossed in the safeguarding of the remnant of their privileges, no serious effort was made to combat the mischief, and in the end Bruges found herself absolutely cut off from the sea. On the other hand, in the enjoyment of peace and the greater security it engendered, Antwerp was slowly asserting herself and gradually attracting to her quays the merchant princes from the littoral of the Zwijn; and as commerce imperceptibly gravitated towards the city by the Scheldt the foreign consuls one by one forsook the doomed emporium of the Hanseatic League. Memling, pursuing the even tenor of his life, continued to produce with unabated ardour and undiminished skill, and with this period – the last fourteen years of his life – is associated the most celebrated of all his works, the marvellous

Shrine of Saint Ursula, the gem of the priceless collection preserved to this day in the old chapter-room of Saint John's Hospital. When this masterpiece was first undertaken we are not in a position to say, but it was completed in 1489, and on the 21st day of October in that year the relics for whose safe keeping it had been designed were deposited within it. But to the eighties belong other memorable productions. In 1484 was finished the interior of the altarpiece for the Moreel chantry in the Church of Saint James, now housed in the Town Gallery at Bruges; in 1487 was painted the portrait of a man preserved in the Gallery of the Offices at Florence, and also was completed the wonderful diptych for Martin van Nieuwenhove, whose portrait we reproduce as the finest example of Memling's work in that particular department of art; and in 1490 the finishing touches were put to the picture in the Louvre of the Madonna and Child, to whom saintly patrons are presenting the family of James Floreins, a younger brother of the donor of the triptych picturing the Adoration of the Magi which, as we have seen, was completed in 1479.

But work, which always spelt happiness to Memling, meant something more to him in this decade of his career. Death in 1487 robbed him of his wife. One pictures to oneself the bereaved artist seeking solace from the grief of his widowed home in intensified application to his art. The refining discipline of sorrow was exercising its softening influence on a nature of whose religious fervour and deep piety his life-work is an abiding testimony. Absorbed in the production of the Shrine of Saint Ursula, does not the instinct of human sympathy suggest to us the artist spending himself in this inimitable work for a monument of his love worthy of the memory of the helpmate who had devoted her life to enhance the happiness of his own, herein seeking and finding surcease of the sorrow that now overshadowed his life, the burden of work balancing the burden of grief? And what a monument! So familiar is the legend and the unique interpretation of it he has left us, one feels it would be a work of supererogation to dwell on the story. But the treatment, viewed by the light of Memling's bereavement, discloses fresh beauties in every panel. Critics have dwelt on the unreality of the death scenes in this shrine. Memling, as we have had sufficient occasion to observe, shrank from the painful expounding of evil. But for him death had no terrors: it was but the passing over to the ineffable reward of a well-spent life, and this innate feeling he conveys to us in the placid acceptance of death by Saint Ursula and her virgin band as but a stepping across the threshold to everlasting bliss. These critics, on the contrary, look for the betrayal of fear and anguish, for the manifestation of human suffering: but, like the martyrs of the early Church, we find these victims of the ruthless Huns not alone meeting their death in a spirit of resignation, but welcoming it with abounding peace and a joyful self-surrender, strong in the hope and faith of the hereafter: as the artist himself was wistfully looking forward to the day and the hour that would reunite him there to the one he had loved best on earth.

Turning to the other works of this period which we have mentioned, the Moreel altarpiece arrests our attention. Apart from the particular friendship which linked him with William Vrelant and the brothers Floreins, few men were more likely to attract him than the donor of this painting. The great-grandson of a Savoyard, Morelli, who had settled in Bruges in 1336, William Moreel, a member of the Corporation of Grocers, after filling various civic offices, was elected burgomaster of Bruges in 1478, and again in the troublous days of 1483. His standing is sufficiently attested by the record that in 1491 only ten of his fellow-citizens were taxed at a higher rate. Able and strong-willed, a capable financier and ardent politician, he was ever foremost in defending the rights and liberties of his country, and to such purpose that Maximilian, who had imprisoned him in 1481, refused when he made his peace with the States of Flanders, on 28th June 1485, to include him in the general amnesty. He retired to Nieuport, but returned to Bruges in 1488 and was chosen as treasurer of the town, and in July 1489 was presented by the magistrates with the sum of £100 in recognition of services rendered. Reference has been made to the independent portraits of Moreel, his wife, and one of his daughters. In the triptych under notice the whole family are gathered together, the father and his five sons, his wife Barbara van Vlaenderberch and their eleven daughters. The donor's head is probably a copy of the Brussels panel, assuming that at the time it was painted, Moreel was still in prison; while that of his wife, more careworn and aged, bears testimony to the anxiety occasioned her by her husband's confinement. This painting, too, will afford the critics who love to find fault with the Flemish school for its alleged inability to do justice to the winsomeness of child life an opportunity of reconsidering their judgment by the light of the Infant Jesus whom Saint Christopher is bearing across the ferry, and once more we are met in every portion of the picture with brilliant exemplifications of the artist's special aptitude for interpreting the beauties of Nature.

Scarcely less attractive, and in some respects even more interesting, is the celebrated diptych associated with the name of Martin van Nieuwenhove. Here we have a departure from Memling's usual practice, which was to present the Blessed Virgin and Child in an open portico, the artist picturing them in a room amply lighted by windows, the upper portions of which are adorned with pictures in stained glass, while the lower halves, mostly thrown open, reveal inimitable scenes of country life; moreover, a convex mirror at the back of Our Lady reflects the depicted scene of the interior. The donor belonged to a noble family long settled in Bruges, evidently a man of great promise, for after being elected a member of the Town Council in 1492, he was chosen burgomaster in 1497 at the early age of thirty-three. Unfortunately he passed away in the prime of life a short three years later. The painting dates from 1487, and the portrait is Memling's masterpiece in that branch of art.

The panel in the Louvre ranks equally with this production, its chief feature being the marvellous grouping of the donors and their family. James Floreins, younger brother of John, the spiritual master of Saint John's Hospital, belonged to one of the wealthiest of the Bruges guilds, the Corporation of Master Grocers, among whose members (John Du Celier and William Moreel to wit) Memling found such generous patrons of his art. He had married a lady of the Spanish Quintanaduena family, who bore him nineteen children: the eldest son, a priest, is represented in furred cassock and cambric surplice, and the second daughter in the habit of a Dominican nun. This picture is another but wholly different departure from the setting usually affected by the artist in his presentment of the Virgin and Child. The throne here is erected in the middle of the nave of a round-arched church, a rood-screen of five bays shutting off the choir. The north transept porch, is adorned with statues of the Prophets, the south portal with others of the Apostles. The difficulty of grouping so large a family in the circumscribed space about the throne is obviated with consummate skill, the father and two eldest sons on the one side, and the mother and two eldest daughters on the other, being placed well in the foreground, while the younger members of either sex are disposed in the aisles, the upstanding figures of Saint James the Great and Saint Dominic beside the throne filling the void on either side which this arrangement entailed. Even here, with the limited opportunities the architectural setting affords, Memling will not be denied his predilection for landscape ornamentation, two delightful glimpses of country life enchanting the eye as it wanders down the transepts and out on to their porches.

If in these pages attention has perhaps been somewhat too exclusively devoted to the portraits of men left us by Memling, obviously enough because of the greater interest they excite by the stories known of their careers, it must not be supposed that he proved himself less skilful as a portrayer of women. As a rule the wives of the donors in his pictures are of the homely type, but they appeal to us none the less as typical examples of the womankind of a burgher community in which the virtues of the home were cherished and sedulously cultivated. Two exceptionally fine specimens of male and female portraiture, which most likely belong to this period, are the bust of an old man in the Royal Museum at Berlin and that of an aged lady, recently acquired by the Louvre for the very substantial sum of 200,000 francs. If, as has been suggested, these are portraits of husband and wife, it is regrettable that they should have strayed so far apart, but the latter we have selected for illustration as perhaps the best available example to demonstrate Memling's aptitude for the interpretation of the dignity of old age in woman.

More amazing perhaps than the magnitude of the work Memling achieved is the dearth of information concerning him that has been vouchsafed to us. Until 1860 nothing whatever was known of the story of his life, and what has been since discovered is almost entirely due to the painstaking researches of one or two individuals. These revealed the fact of Memling's marriage, the name of the woman he chose for his wife and that of her father, the fact that she bore him three sons – John, Cornelius, and Nicolas – the year of his wife's death, the record of house property bought by him, the date of his own death and his place of burial, and this is the sum total of the material at our disposal, apart from his paintings, with which to build up his biography. The Shrine that is his masterpiece once completed, the only other dated work of which we have any knowledge is the polyptych altarpiece which hangs in the Greverade chantry of the Cathedral at Lubeck. This bears on its frame the date 1491; but the execution of the painting is very unequal, and it appears probable that the greater part is the work of pupils. Perhaps Memling felt that he had lived his life, and was content to lay aside palette and brush in the consciousness that he had given the world of his best. Maybe, too, as the years began to tell, there grew a yearning for the privacy of home life in more intimate communion with the motherless children from whom he himself was soon to be parted. All too speedily the end came, for he passed away on the 11th of August 1494, at a ripe old age considering the average length of days meted out to man in his time.

VII

EFFACEMENT AND
VINDICATION OF HIS TYPES

BRUGES, the scene of his stupendous lifework and his home for
nearly the last thirty years of his life, was fast settling down to
utter stagnation and the general poverty it superinduced. One
needs to realise the measure of her decay to understand the
possibility of such a personality as Memling's fading from the
public memory. True, he had founded no school to perpetuate his
art and cherish his name and reputation. Twice we find mention
of apprentices in the register of the Guild of Painters – a John
Verhanneman, inscribed on 8th May 1480, and a Passchier Van
der Meersch, in 1483. Neither attained the rank of master-painter.
Nor is it known that any of the three sons inherited their father's
talent or followed his profession. However, we remember that
Rumwold De Doppere, writing of his death in the year it
occurred, asserted that he was "then considered to be the most
skilful and excellent painter in the whole of Christendom," while
Van Vaernewyck, as late as 1562, tells of the houses of Bruges
being still filled with paintings by Memling among other great
artists. And yet so completely was he forgotten within a century of
his death that Van Mander, when preparing his biographies of

Netherlandish painters (published in 1604), could only learn that he was in his day "a celebrated master who flourished before the time of Peter Pourbus" – that is, before 1540! Neglect and disdain followed speedily on forgetfulness, and the scattering of his priceless works commenced. The magnificent picture of the Passion of Christ in the Turin Museum, which adorned the altar of the chapel of the Guild of Saint John and Saint Luke in the Church of Saint Bartholomew until 1619, was then removed to a side wall, and five years later sold to make room for an organ! The no less famous painting "Christ the Light of the World," which graced the altar of the chapel of the Guild of Tanners in the Church of Our Lady until 1764, was then removed to the house of the dean, who a few years later sold it to a picture-dealer at Antwerp for 20 *l.*! And so these masterpieces were made the sport and spoil of picture-dealers and traffickers in curiosities. Under Spanish rule further toll was levied on the art treasures of Bruges, and of what escaped the vulgar vandalism of the Calvinists, whose utter inability to create was only equalled by their senseless capacity for destruction, the French revolutionaries, whose sense of the beautiful in art not all their irreligion had sufficed to stifle, claimed a considerable share. Fortunately the ultimate defeat of Napoleon made restitution in a measure possible, and so the Moreel triptych, seized on 23rd August 1794, and the Van Nieuwenhove diptych, carried off in the same month, were recovered in 1815. Still the fact remains that Bruges at this date possesses only seven of Memling's works. The remainder are dispersed among the galleries of the Continent – in Brussels and Antwerp; in Paris; in Madrid; in Rome, Florence, Turin, and Venice; in Vienna and Buda-Pesth; in Berlin, Frankfort, Munich, Danzig, Lubeck, Hermannstadt, and Woerlitz; and at the Hague; while England boasts of three pictures, two in the National Gallery and one at Chatsworth.

Although Memling founded no school, the masters of his day and others who settled in Bruges in the sixteenth century were to a very appreciable extent influenced by his art. Gerard David,

Albert Cornelis, Peter Pourbus, and the Claeissens all felt its impress, and if the traditions of the old school survived in Bruges to a later period than in other centres, and well into the seventeenth century, it was mainly through the instrumentality of these painters. In contrasting the lives of mediæval and modern artists one cannot escape a feeling of regret that the former should so utterly have neglected the literary side of their calling. What a revelation to us would have been the discovery of the personal recollections of but one of these great masters of the fifteenth and sixteenth centuries, and what a world of trouble they would have saved the art students of after generations! But seemingly the demand for this class of literature had not then arisen, while the craving for notoriety which would have compelled an effort of this description was altogether foreign to the single-minded nature of a school whose art was to its exponents something more than the realisation of worldly ambition or the satisfaction of a vulgar lust of gain. There could have been no hankering after either in the type of man revealed to us by the lifework of Memling. And so it was that with the reawakened interest in mediæval painting which made itself manifest in the nineteenth century the services of the archæologist had to be requisitioned. Difficult indeed would it be to exaggerate the immensity of the task imposed upon him. The sifting from the mass of popular fiction which had gathered round Memling's name the few grains of truth embedded in it, the ceaseless delving among municipal and ecclesiastical archives for a chance record of some incident in his career, the slow process of authenticating the genuine from the ruck of doubtful and spurious works associated with his name, half a century of unswerving devotion to the task has not yet brought us within measurable reach of its accomplishment. Every day, so to speak, brings to light some new fact, often compelling a revision of conclusions which in its absence were sufficiently justified.

Thus it happened that the identification of the donors of the "Last Judgment" at Danzig, in 1902, led to the recognition of this earliest example of Memling's art. And so no doubt will it happen again, each fresh discovery amplifying the knowledge necessary to remove doubt as to the authenticity of attributed works. But even so, what an advance from half a century since, when the personality of the painter was but the sport of idle legend, and loomed vaguely on the horizon in the distorted outlines of a loathsome caricature! If dearth of information is a powerful incentive to the imagination, then the evolution of the Memling legend goes far to establish its potency. An obscure seventeenth-century tradition had it that Memling painted a picture for the Hospital of Saint John in grateful recognition of services rendered to him by the Brethren of that charitable foundation: from which indeterminate report grew a tale of a dissolute soldier of fortune spared from the shambles of the field of Nancy dragging his wounded and diseased body to the Hospital gates, and beguiling the weary hours of a long convalescence there in the production of a masterpiece of painting in token of his gratitude. As an unconnected story for the amusement of simple-minded folk the fable is not without merit of a sort, but what a libel on the Christian artist who transcends all the painters of his age in the interpretation of deep religious feeling, and the shaping of whose whole life must have been a novitiate to this end! We have travelled a long road since the days when this preposterous legend was exploded. True, the exhumation of Memling's individuality from the burial-ground of lost memories has been a slow and arduous process; but the rich store of knowledge now at our command is an abundant testimony to the patience of the experts who have garnered it.

It is not given to us to be all swayed in the same way or to the same extent by Art in any of its forms; but few who have been led to contemplate the masterpieces of the Netherlandish school will fail to pay the tribute of admiration these wonderworks evoke, and bear testimony to their educational value. For Hans Memling it is not claimed that he surpassed in each department of his art all the other painters who helped to build up the fame of the Netherlandish school: in some material respects his methods differed widely from theirs, and he elaborated a technique distinctly his own. It is not likely to be imputed that his sedulous avoidance of the marked contrasts of light and shade was a confession of inability to realise their treatment, though possibly he may be thought by some to have weakly followed the line of least resistance. Of course, Memling, like every other great artist of his age, had his limitations. His knowledge of anatomy naturally was not equal to the exact requirements of science, the pose of his figures not absolutely conformable to the ideals of the dilettante in respect of grace of carriage or correctness of deportment. Though critics contrast the simplicity of his art with the grandeur of style of Van Eyck, commonly with some predilection for the latter, yet it is possible for one to be subjugated by it and still feel to the full the fascination of the tender beauty inherent in the former. In his conceptions of the great mysteries of the Christian faith, in the characterisation of the many saints he portrayed, and above all in his varied presentation of womanhood he certainly excelled. In the "Last Judgment" at Danzig we have probably the least successful of his great efforts. The conception is not original, though admittedly one of the finest produced up to that time; also it is his earliest extant work, and in the style of a master from whose controlling influence he had not yet emancipated himself. But the fault lies rather with the subject. Many an artist has laboured at it, not always perhaps from choice; but the painter has yet to be born who will produce a convincing picture of that unrealised tragedy. Any attempt that falls short of conveying to the mind and soul of man the awe-full warning it should express necessarily bears the stamp of failure; and when, as too often is the case, it but provokes a smile by reason of its incongruity, the effort it cost stands unjustified. Not that Memling's conception errs conspicuously in this sense: but it lacks conviction, and not all the beautiful work it exhibits can close our eyes to the fact.

To the up-to-date art critic of the weekly press, steeped in modernity, all this grand religious art of the middle ages is but as the dead ashes of a fire that once glowed but has now lost its warmth; or, to vary the simile, he contemptuously relegates it to the scrap-heap of antiquated material as the useless remains of a "dead language"; little bethinking himself of the great underlying truth he was unconsciously voicing. For just as all succeeding literatures found their spring and inspiration in the magnificent literatures enshrined in the great dead languages of Rome and Greece, so likewise has modern art, unconsciously if you will, but none the less assuredly, derived the essence of its loveliness from the mediæval art it affects to despise. Art of any kind to be great must have realised its greatness through the vivifying power of the art that had gone before. *Ex nihilo nihil fit.* The impellent craving after realism of the materialistic school of to-day is but a perverted form of the love of truth which was the keynote of all mediæval art, its cult of the sensuous but a depraved phase of a love of the beauty in virtue and godliness which characterised the latter: the great touch of faith is wholly wanting. In art as in all things human there is no finality; but the while Bruges subsists, though she were utterly bereft of all her picturesqueness and the wealth of architectural beauty that endears her to the artist mind, so long will that treasure-house of Memling's art, the small chapter-room in the Hospital of Saint John, continue to exercise its educating influence, and so long, because of it, will the old Flemish capital, though shorn of all its pristine glory, continue to be one of the most cherished shrines of the art pilgrims of the world.

On the following pages are some works by contemporaries of Hans Memling.

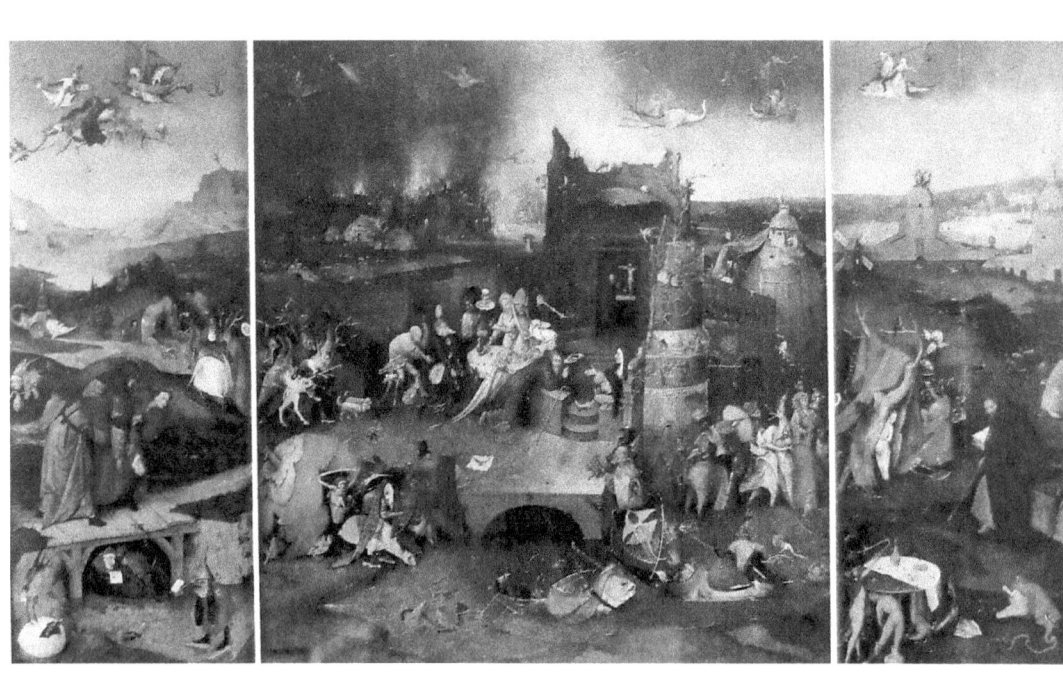

Hieronymous Bosch, The Temptations of St Anthony

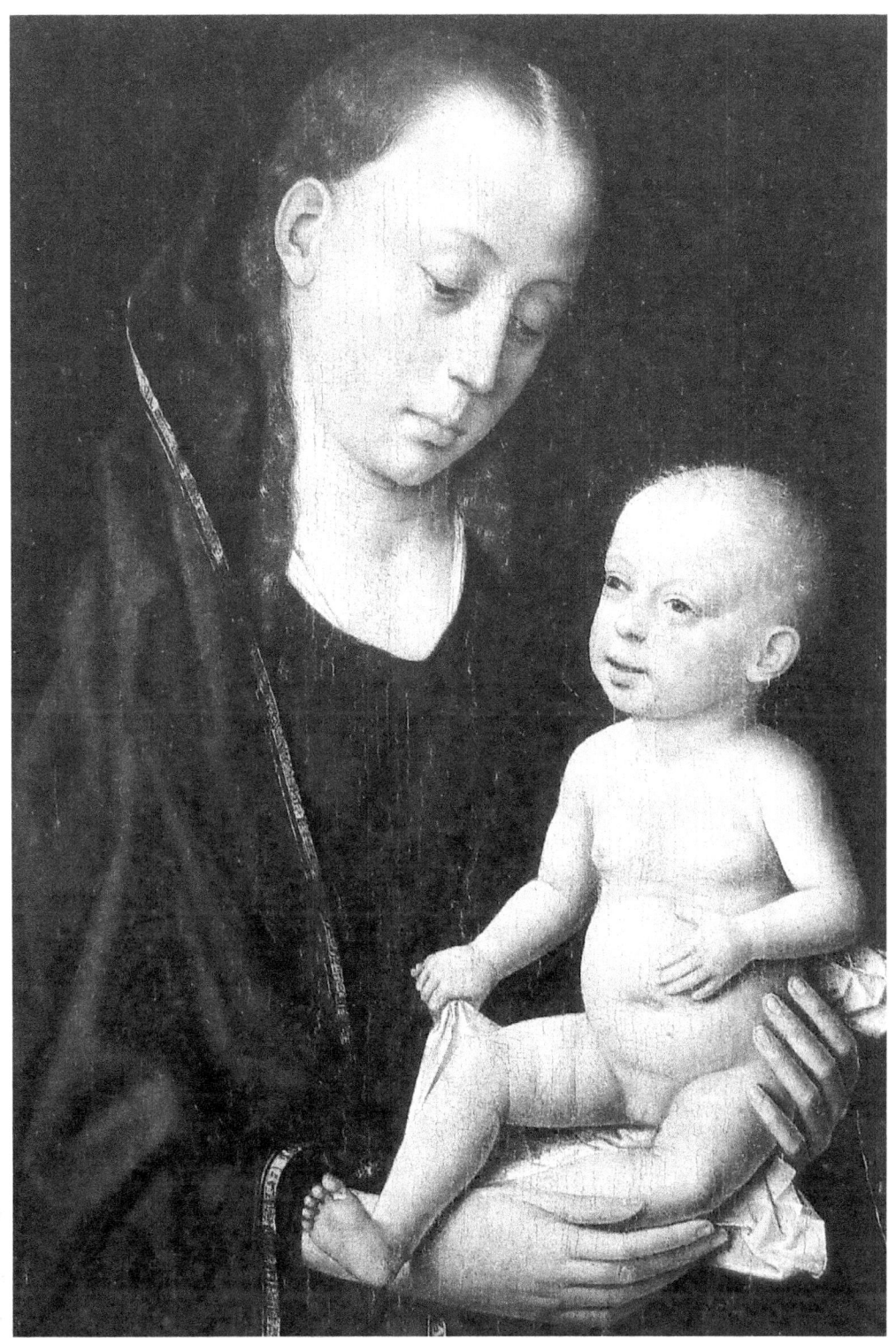

Dieric Bouts, Virgin and Child, National Gallery of Art, Washington, DC

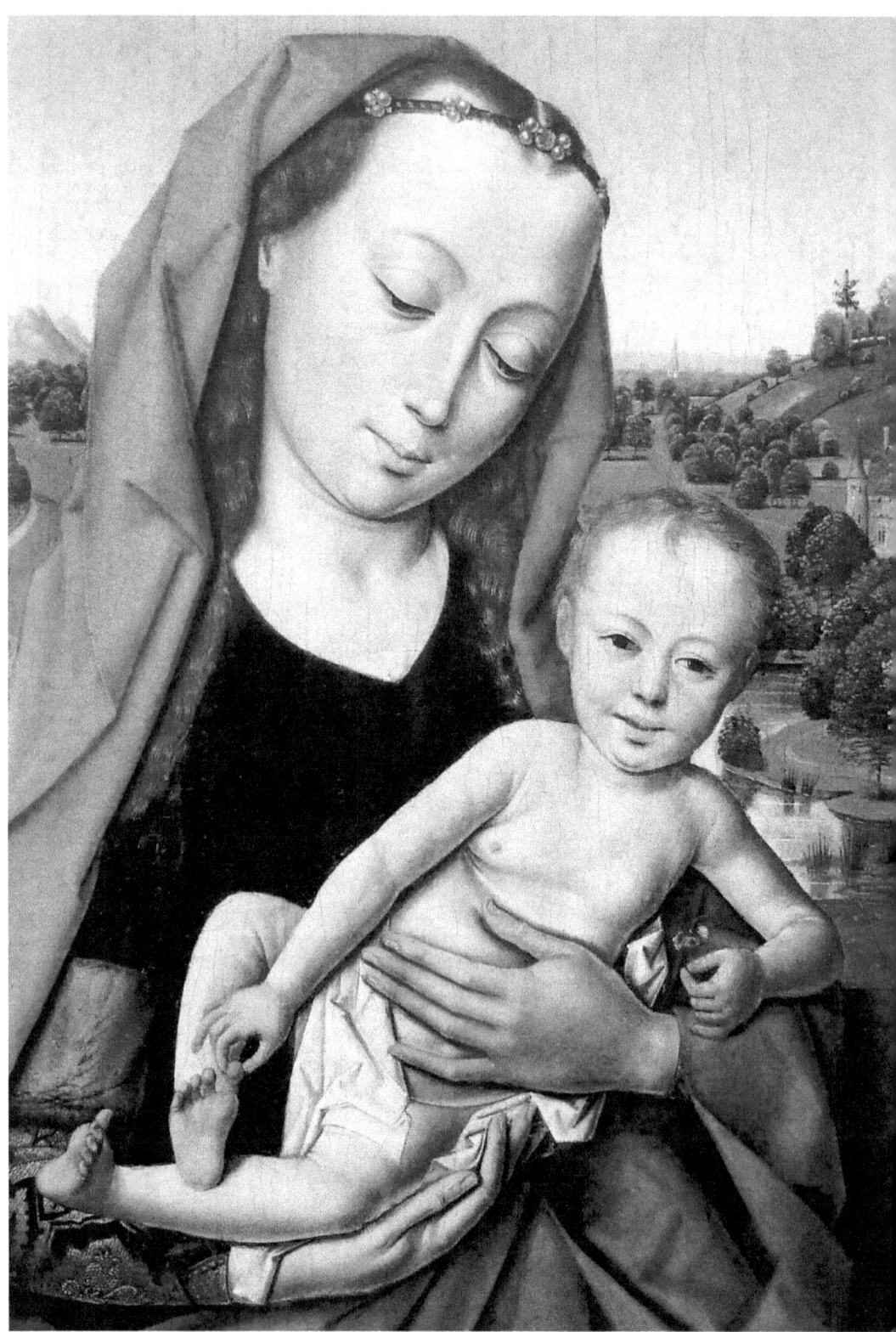
Dieric Bouts (workshop), Virgin and Child, Metropolitan Museum, New York City

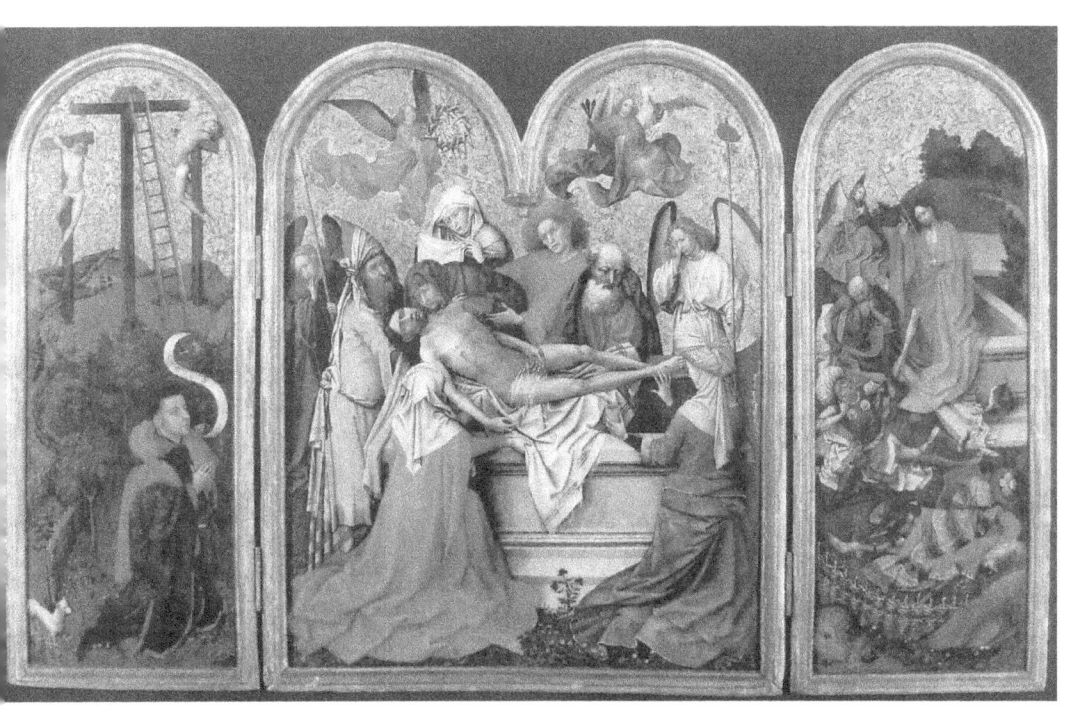

Robert Campin, Seilern Triptych, Courtlauld Institute, London

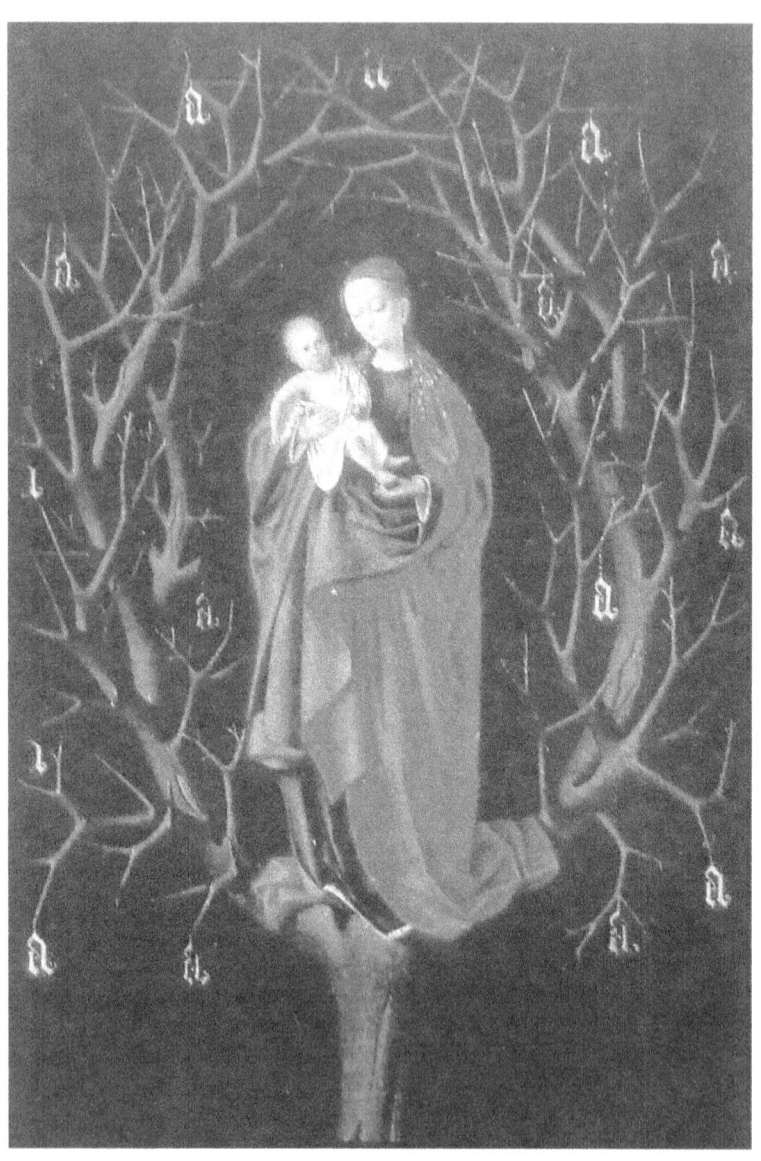

Petrus Christus, Madonna In a Barren Tree, 1450,
Prado, Madrid

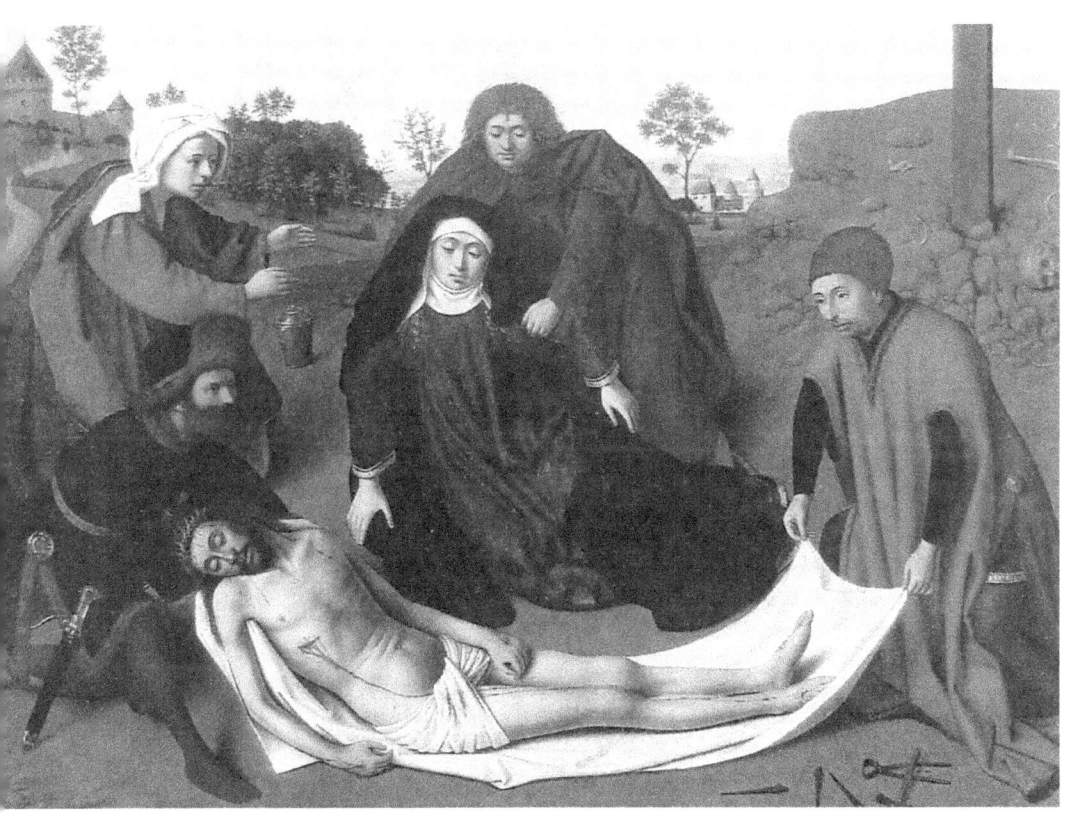

Petrus Christus, The Lamentation, Metropolitan Museum,
New York City

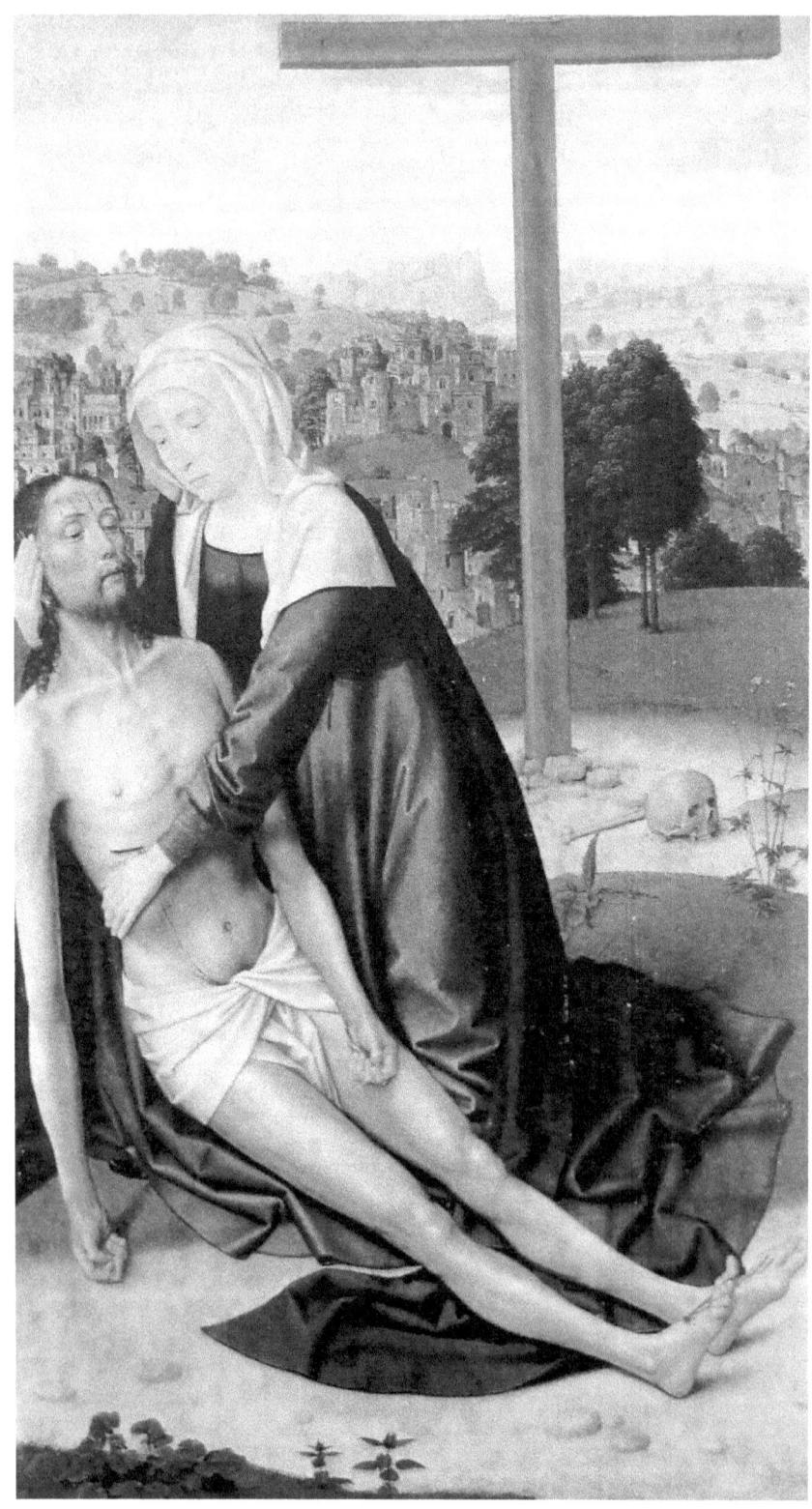

Gerard David, Pietà, Winterhur

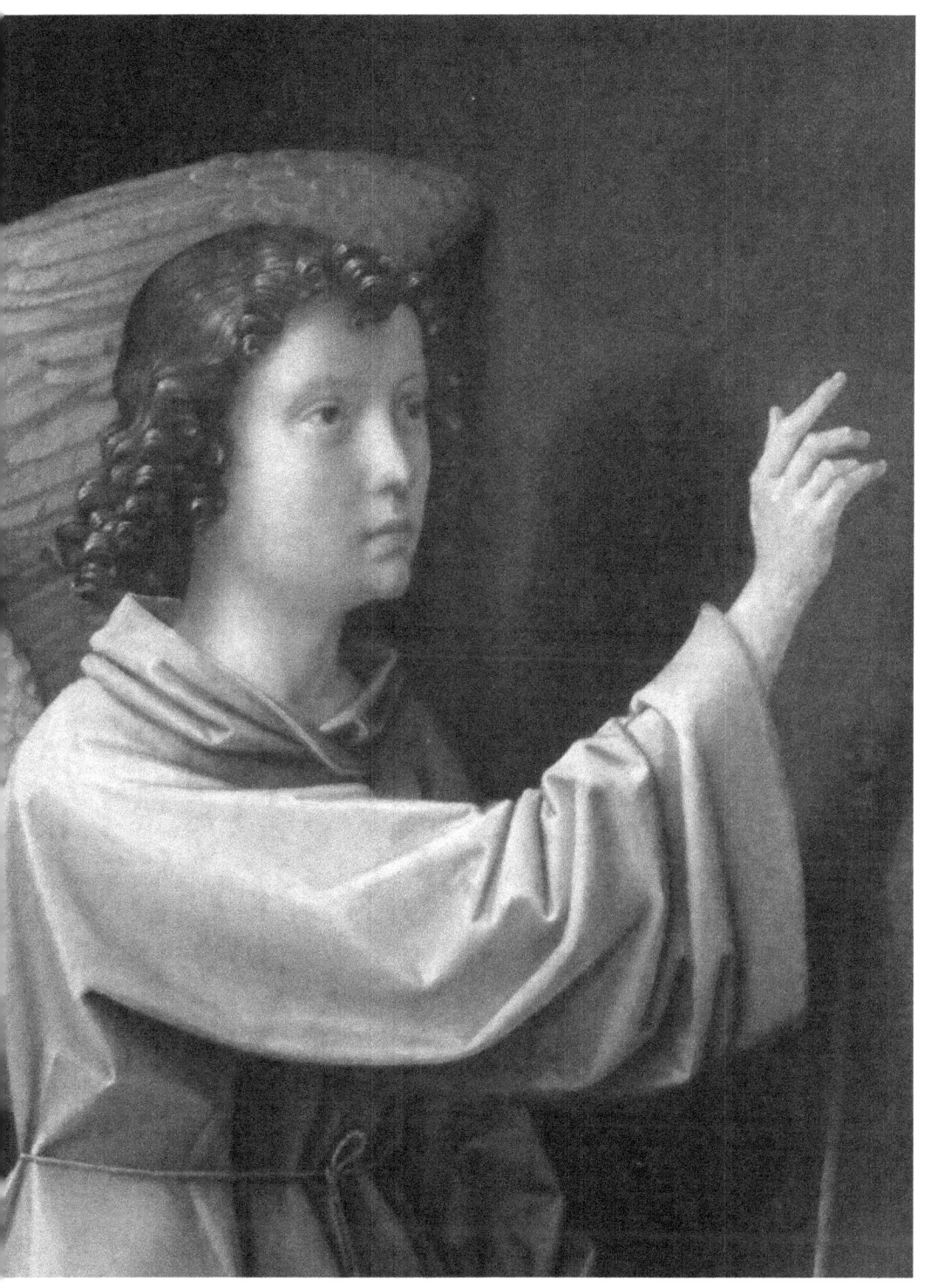

Gerard David in the Metropolitan Museum of Art

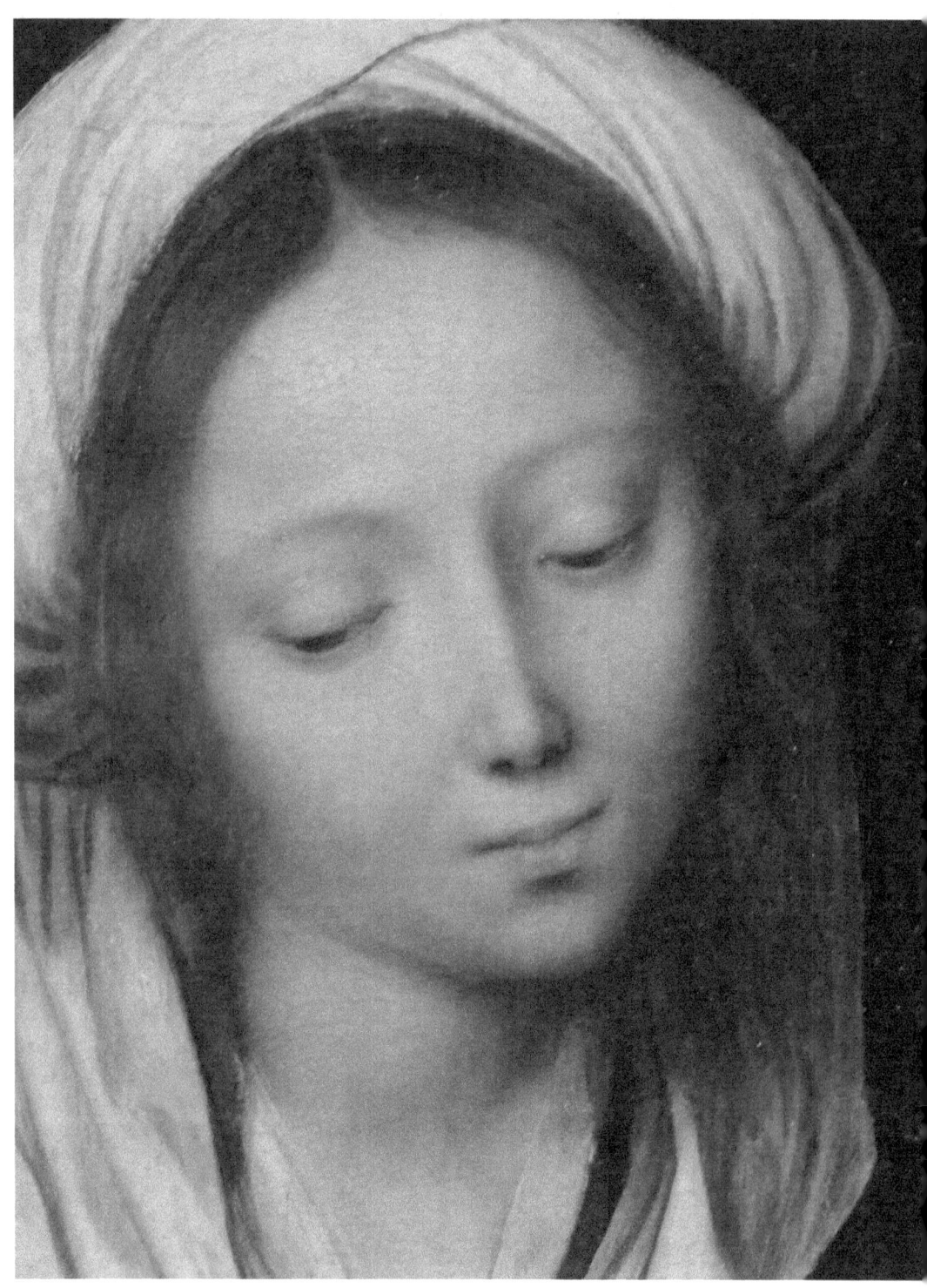

Gerard David, detail of the Adoration, Metropolitan Museum of Art

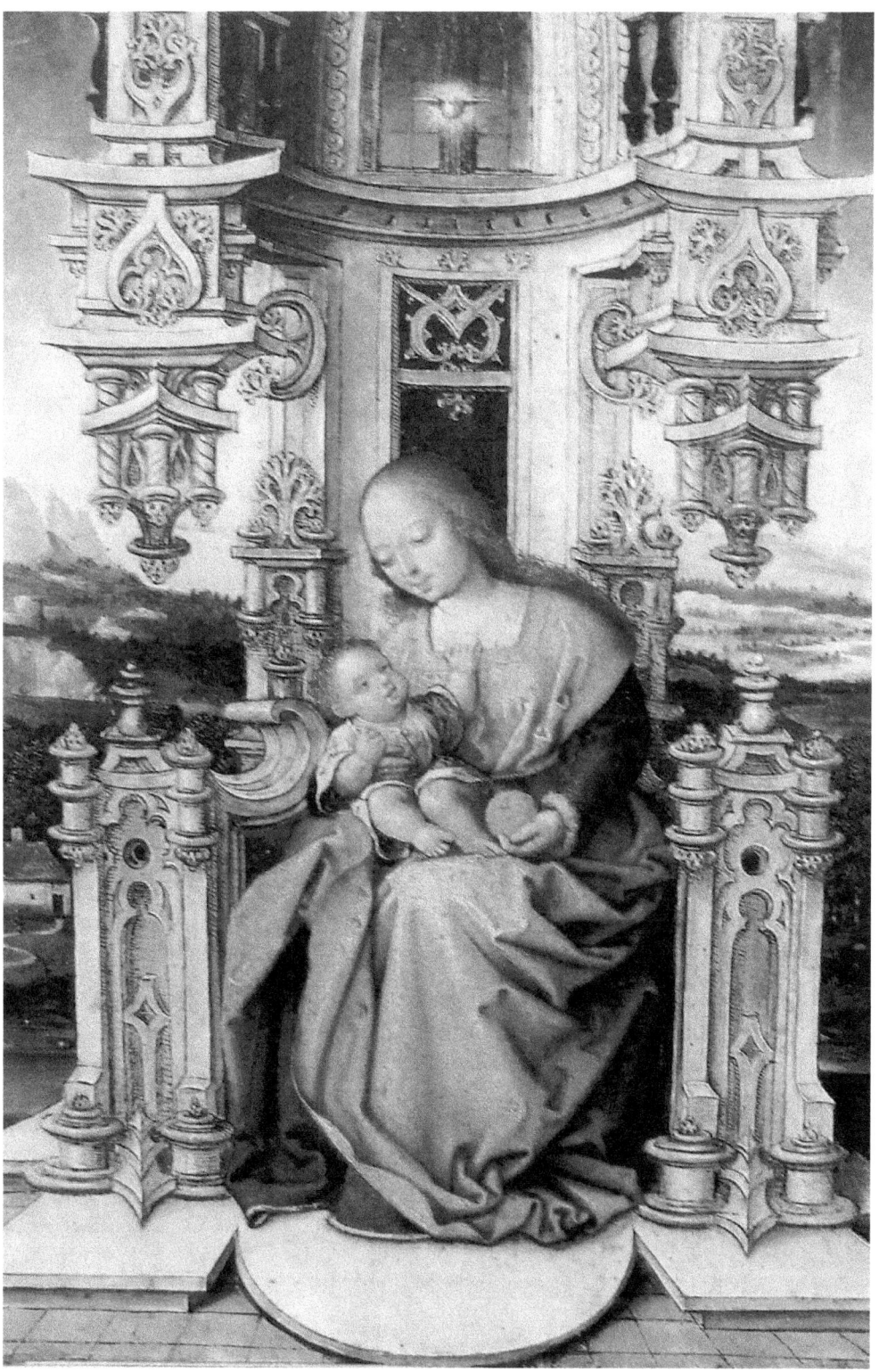

Jan Gossaert, Madonna and Child, Antwerp

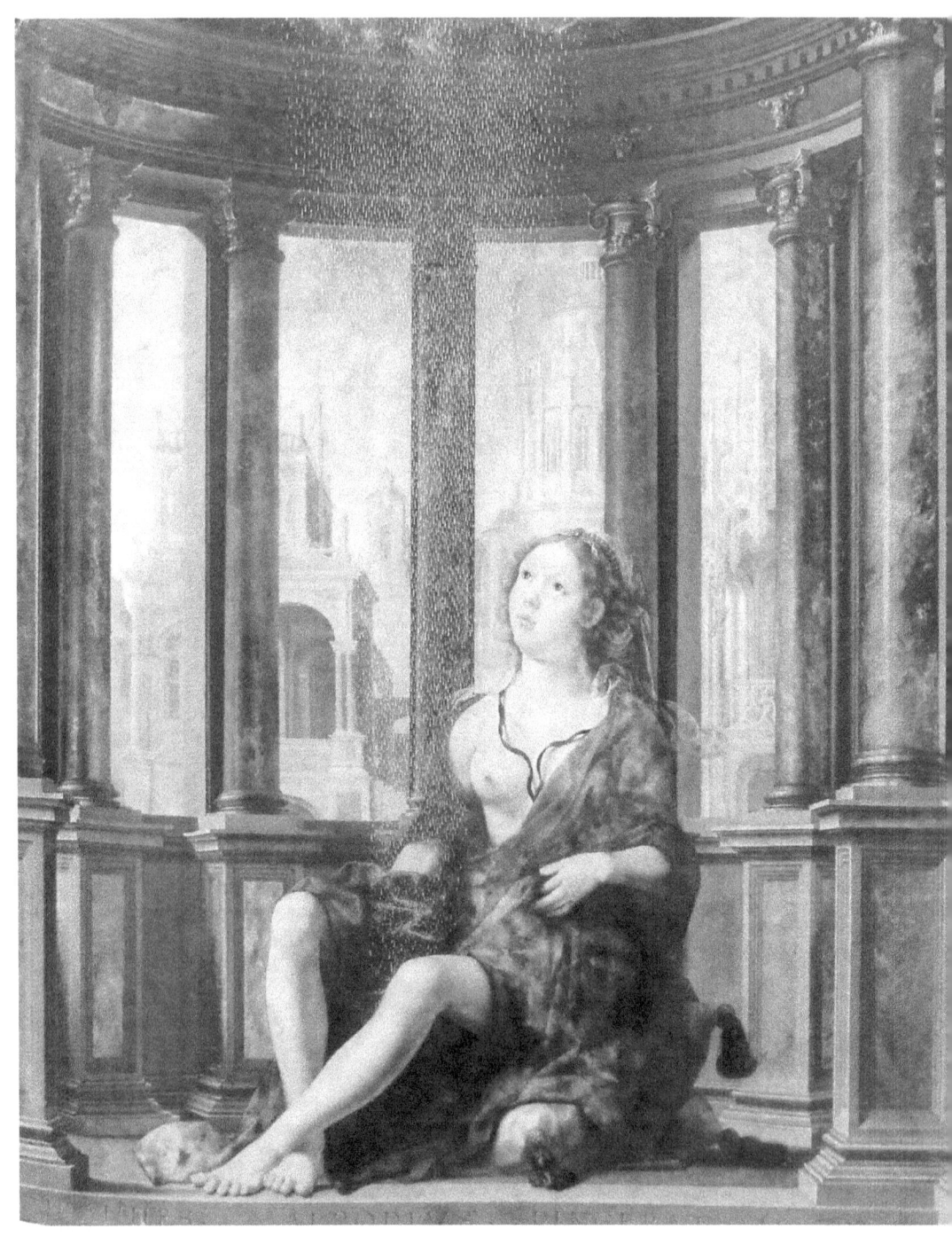

Jan Gossaert (Mabuse), Danae, Munich

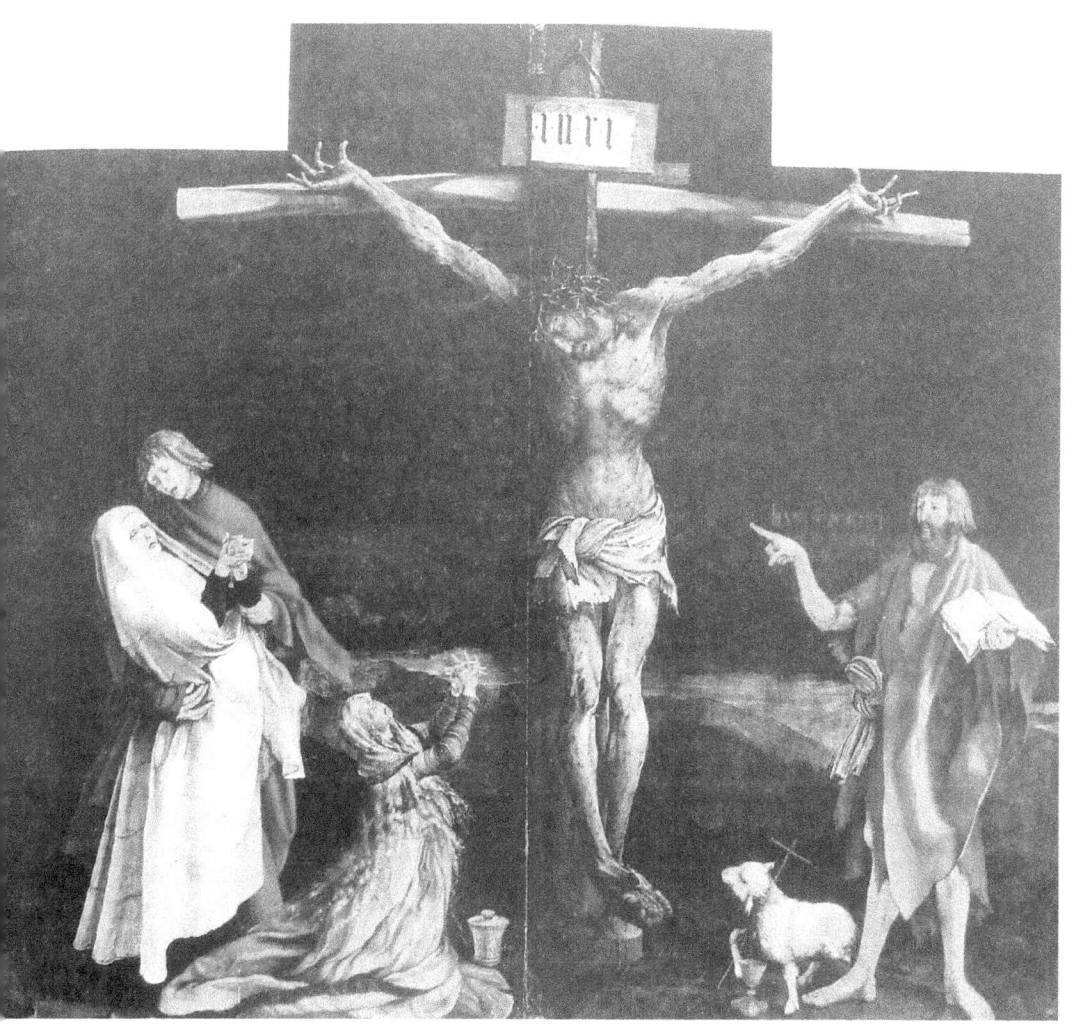

Matthias Grünewald, Crucifixion, Isenheim Altarpiece

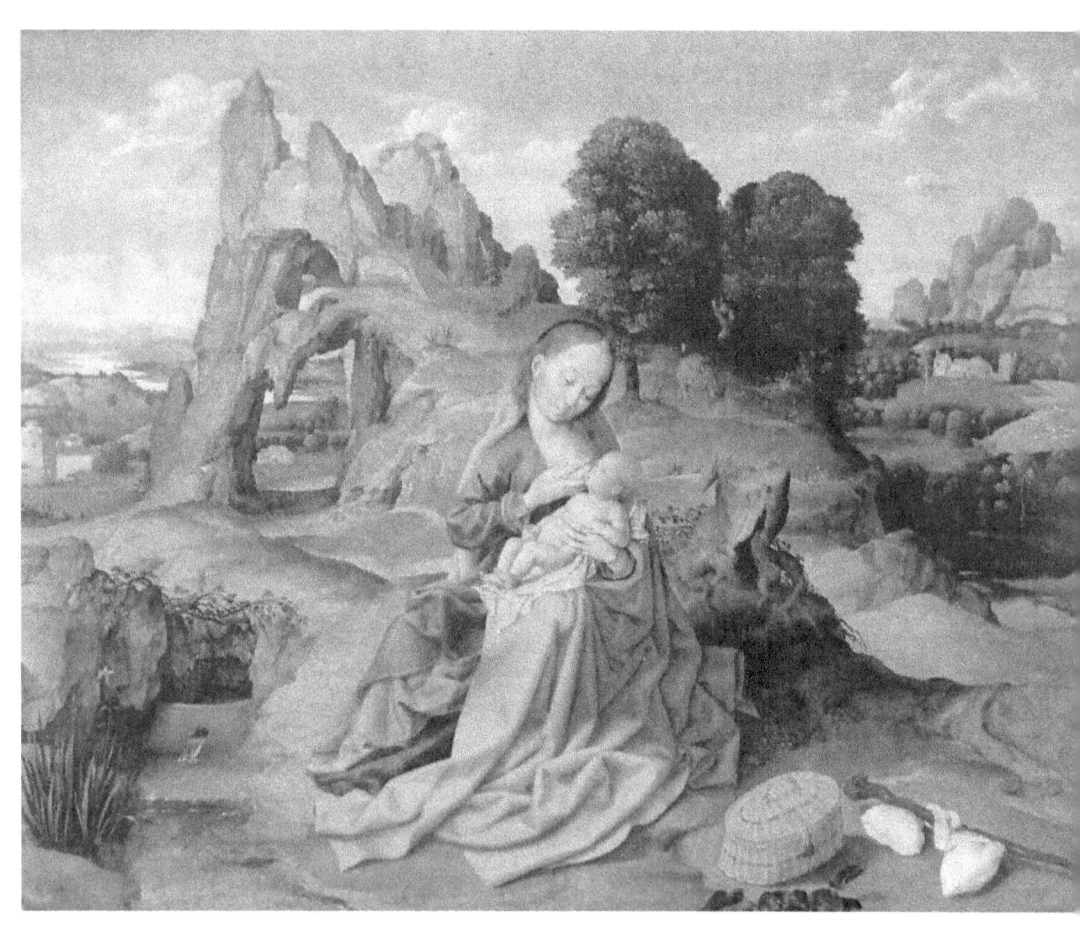

Joos van Cleve, The Rest on the Flight To Egypt, Brussels

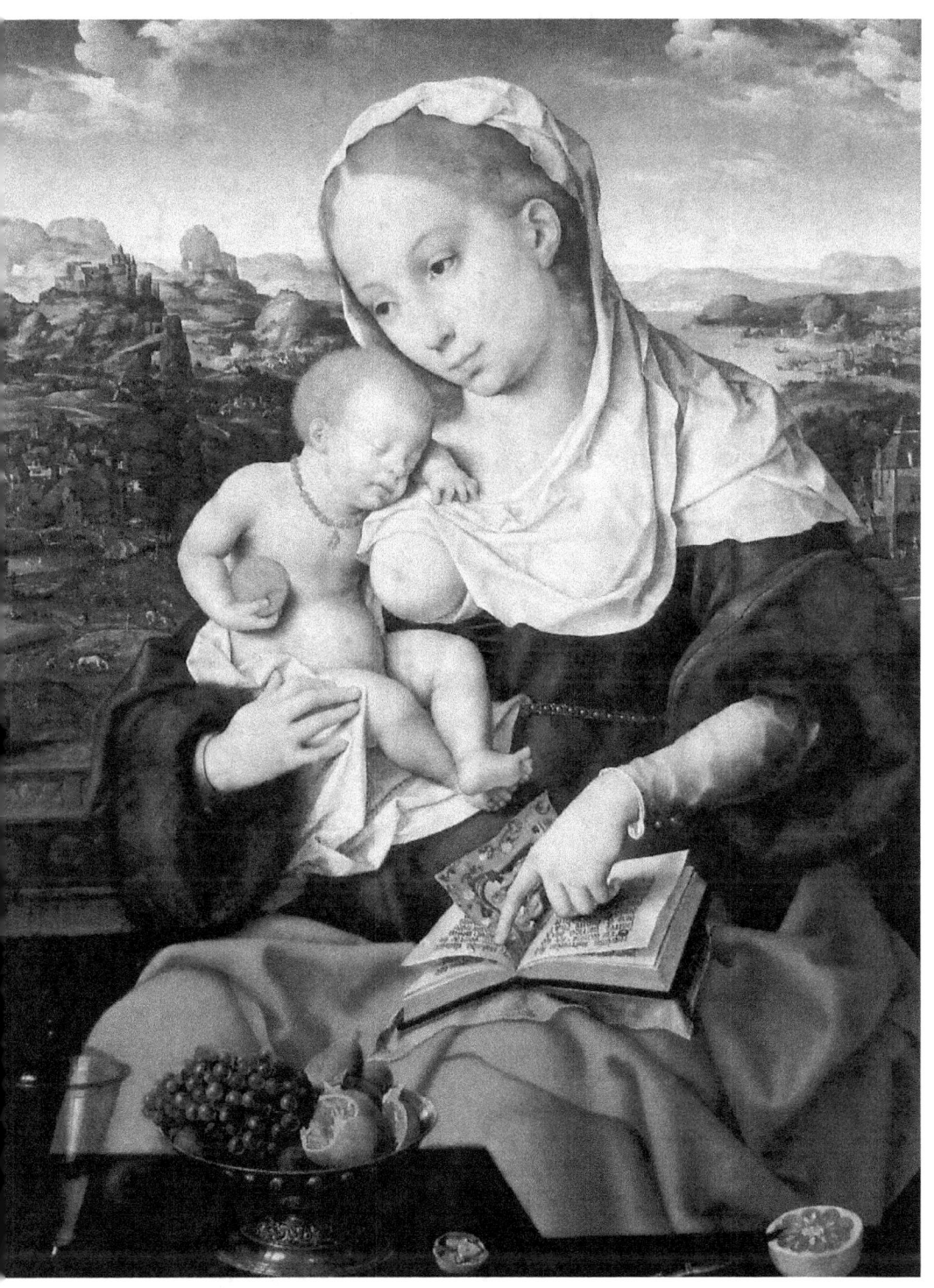

Joos van Cleve, Madonna and Child, Metropolitan Museum,
New York City

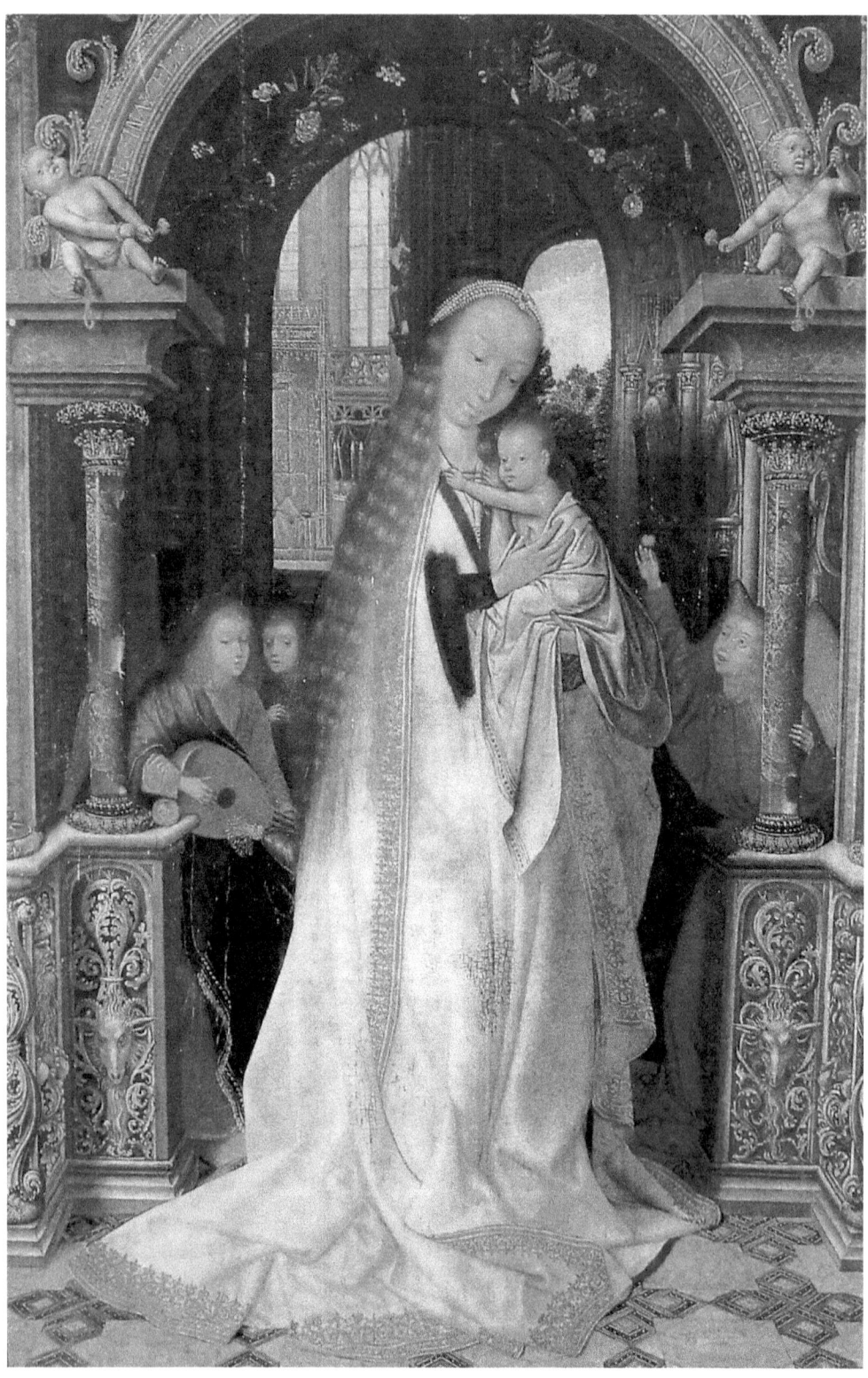

Quentin Massys, The Virgin Standing, With Angels, Lyons

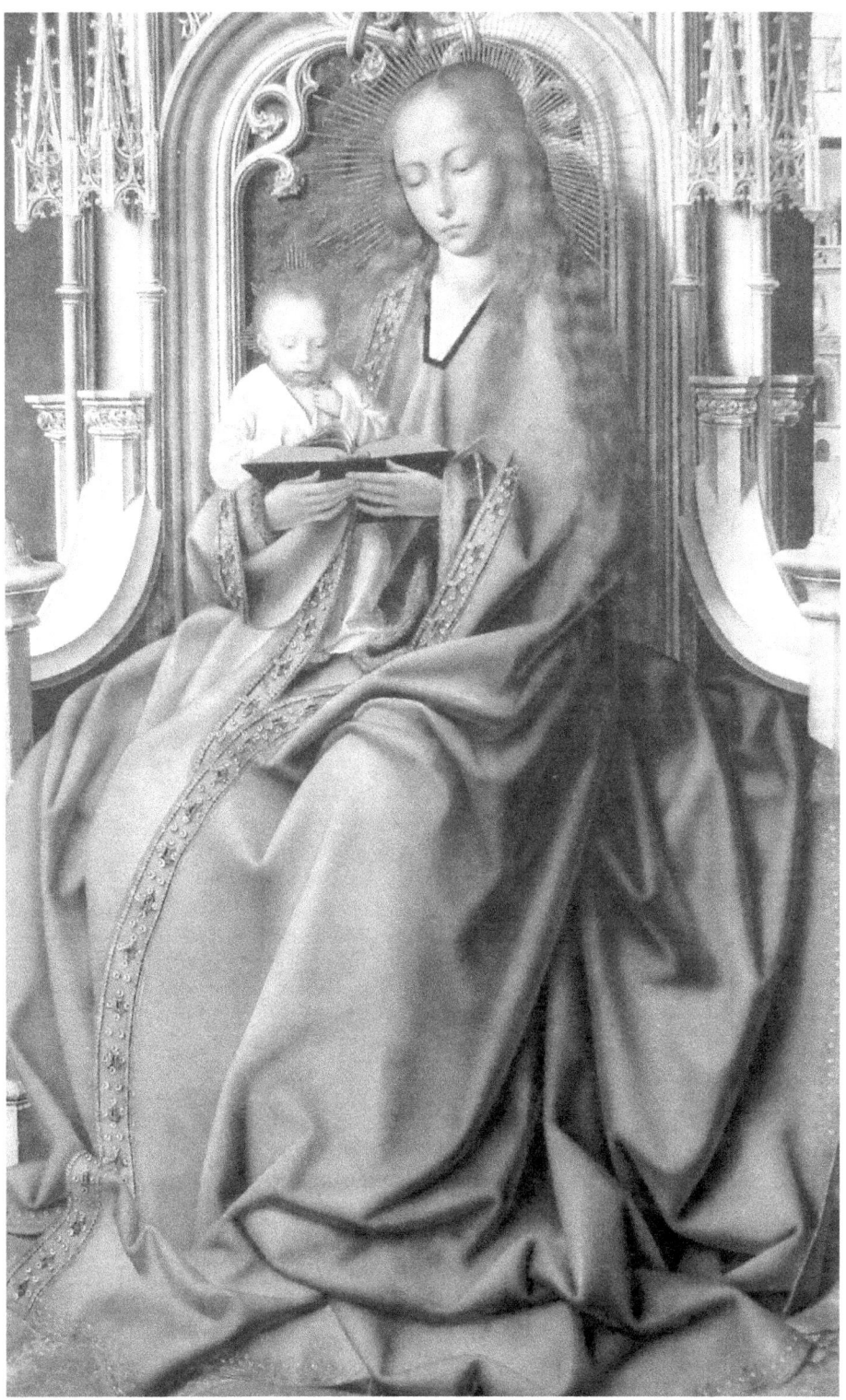

Quentin Massys, Madonna and Child Enthroned, Brussels

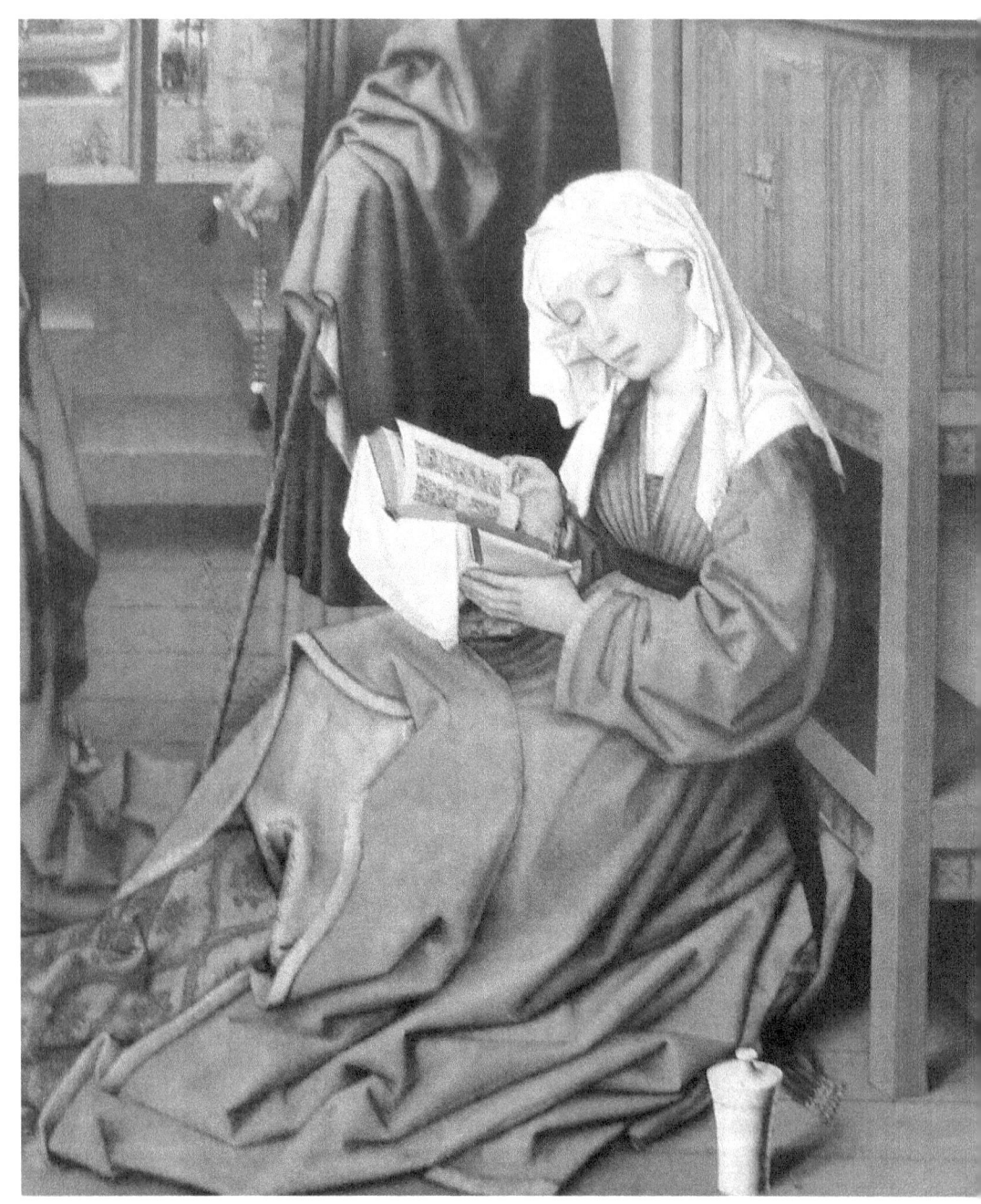

Rogier van der Weyden, Mary Magdalene Reading, detail, National Gallery, London

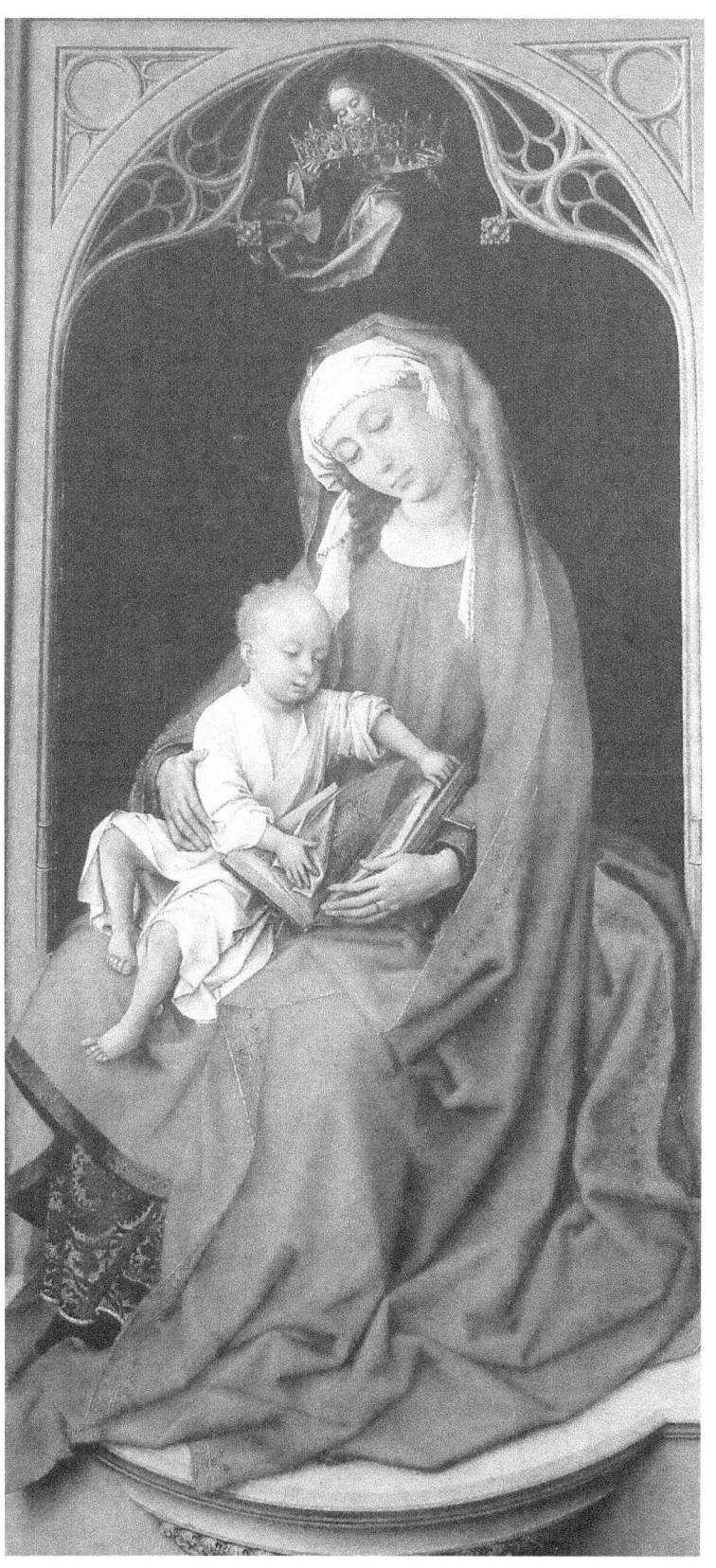

Rogier van der Weyden, Madonna and Child, Prado, Madrid

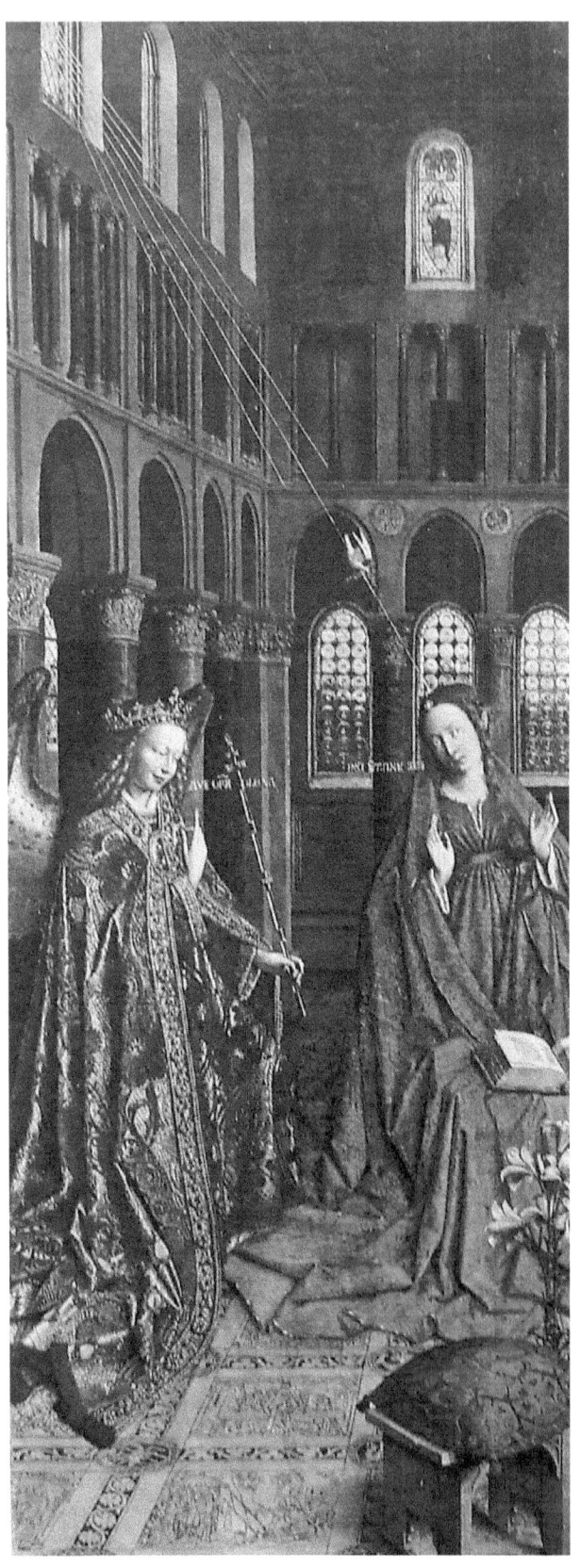

Jan van Eyck, The Annunciation, National Gallery of Art, Washington, DC

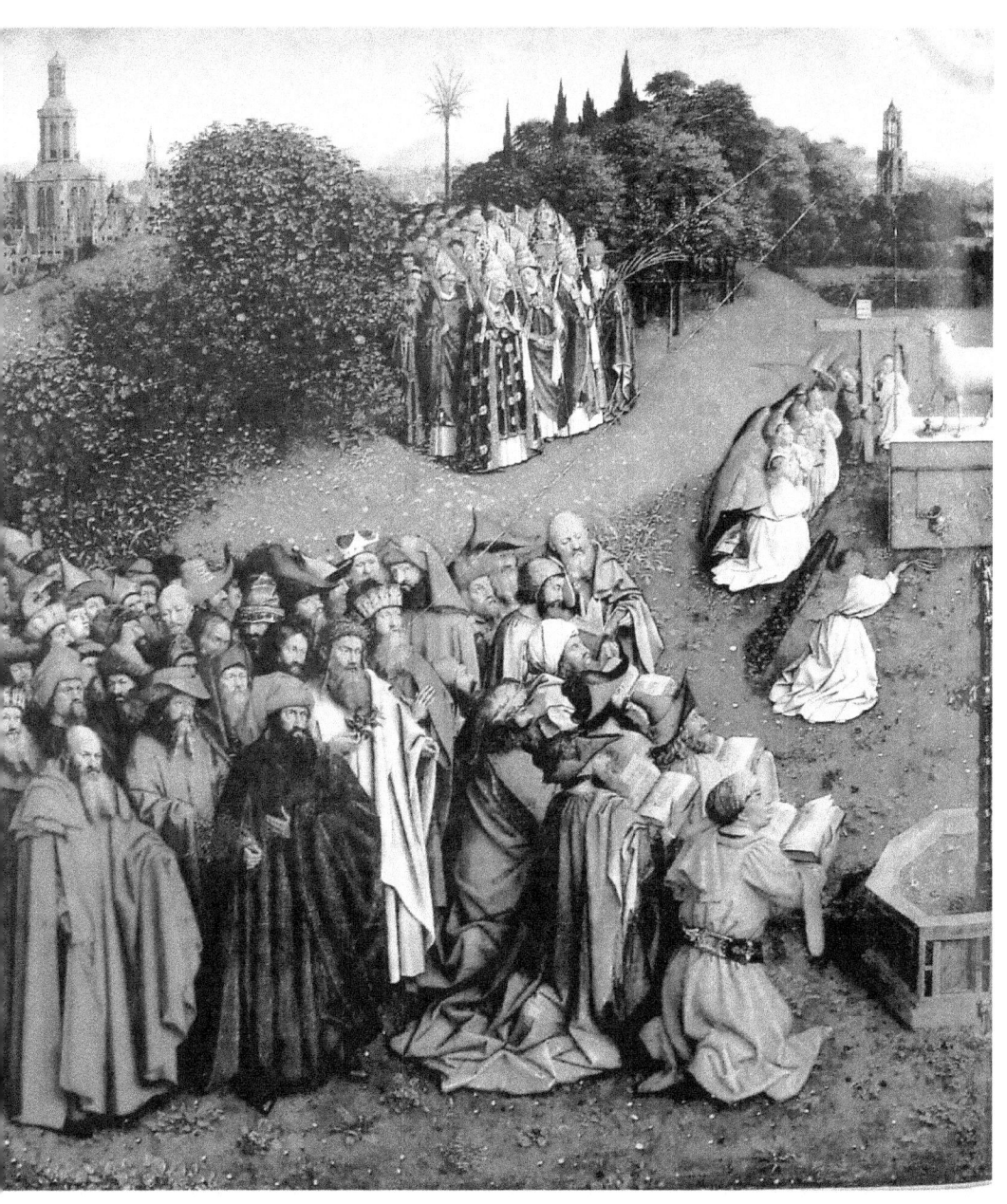

Jan van Eyck, The Ghent Altarpiece, detail

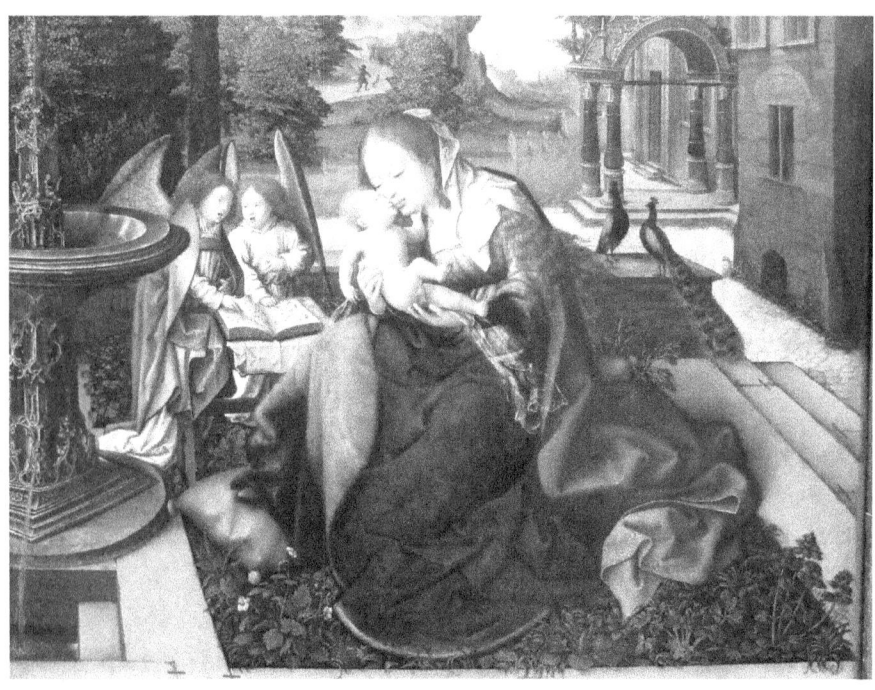

Bernard Van Orley. Madonna and Child,
Metropolitan Museum of Art, New York

BIBILIOGRAPHY

Maryan W. Ainsworth: *Petrus Christus: Renaissance Master of Bruges*, Metropolitan Museum of Art, New York/ Harry N. Abrams, 1994

F. Ames-Lewis: "Fra Filippo Lippi and Flanders", *Zeitschrift für Kunstgeschichte*, XLII, 1979, 255-273

Emile de Antonio & Mitch Tuchman: *Painters Painting*, Abbeville Press, New York 1984

C.G. Argan: *The Renaissance*, Thames & Hudson 1969

Karen Armstrong: *The Gospel According to Woman; Christianity's Creation of the Sex War in the West*, Pan 1987

Geoffrey Ashe: *The Virgin: Mary's Cult and the Re-emergence of the Goddess*, Arkana 1987

—. *Discovering the Goddess: A Personal Testimony*, Crescent Moon 2007

Patrick Bade: *Femme Fatale: Images of evil and fascinating women*, Ash & Grant 1979

Ludwig van Baldass: *Jan van Eyck*, London 1952

Michael Baxandall: *Painting and Experience in 15th Century Italy*, Oxford University Press 1988

—. *Patterns of Intention: On the Historical Explanation of Pictures*, Yale University Press 1985

Germain Bazin: "Petrus Christus et les rapports entre l'Italie et la flandre au milieu du xve siècle", *Revue des Arts*, II, 1952

James Beck: *Italian Renaissance Painting*, Harper & Row, New York 1981

Ean Begg: *The Cult of the Black Virgin*, Routledge 1985

Hans Beltin & Dagmar Eichberger: *Jan van Eyck als Erzähler*, Worms 1983

Bernard Berenson: *The Italian Painters of the Renaissance*, Phaidon 1952/ Fontana 1960

—. *Looking at Pictures with Bernard Berenson*, selected by Hann Kiel,

Abrams, New York 1974

Pamela Berger: *The Goddess Obscured*, Robert Hale 1988

Bruce Bernard: *The Queen of Heaven: A Selection of Painting the Virgin from the Twelfth to the Eighteenth Centuries*, Macdonald/ Orbis 1987

—. *The Bible and Its Painters*, Orbis 1983

Carlo Bertelli: *Piero della Francesca,* Yale University Press, New Haven 1992

Jan Bialostocki: *Jan van Eyck*, Warsaw 1973

K.M. Birkmeyer: "The Arch Motif in Netherlandish Painting in the 15th Century", *Art Bulletin*, 43, June 1961

Shirley Nielsen Blum: "Symbolic Invention in the Art of Rogier van der Weyden", *Konsthistorisk tidskrift*, XLVI, 1977

—. *Early Netherlandish Triptychs: A Study in Patronage*, Berkeley 1969

Charles Bouleau: *The Painter's Secret Geometry: A Study of Composition in Art*, tr. Jonathan Griffin, Thames & Hudson 1963

Serge Bramly: *Leonardo: The Artist and the Man*, Michael Joseph 1992

Allan Brahama: *Italian Renaissance Painters of the Sixteenth Century*, National Gallery 1985

Helmut Brinker: *Zen in the Art of Painting*, Routledge & Kegan Paul 1987

Stephanie Brown: *Religious Painting*, Phaidon 1979

J. Bruyn: *Van Eyck Problemen*, Utrecht 1957

Jacob Burckhardt: *The Altarpiece in Renaissance Italy*, Phaidon 1988

Titus Burckhardt: *Sacred Art in East and West*, Perennial Book, Middlesex 1967

Anne Hagopian van Buren: "The Canonical Office in Renaissance Painting, Part II: More About the Rolin Madonna", *Art Bulletin*, LX, 1978

Caroline Walker Bynum: "The Body of Christ in the Later Middle Ages: A Reply to Leo Steinberg", *Renaissance Quarterly*, XXIX, 1986

Robert Cafritz *et al*: *Places of Delight: The Pastoral Landscape,* Weidenfeld & Nicolson 1989

Ritchie Calder: *Leonardo and The Age of the Eye*, Heinemann 1970

Joseph Campbell: *The Power of Myth*, with Bill Moyers, ed. Betty Sue Flowers, Doubleday, New York 1988

Lorne Campbell: *Van der Weyden*, New York 1980

—"Robert Campin, the Master of Flémalle and the Master of Mérode", *Burlington Magazine*, CXVI, 1974

Michael P. Carroll: *The Cult of the Virgin Mary*, Princeton University Press, New Jersey 1986

Richard Cavendish: *Visions of Heaven and Hell*, Orbis 1977

Andre Chastel: *Art of the Italian Renaissance*, tr. Peter & Linda Murray, Alpine Fine Arts Collection 1985

—. *The Studios and Styles of the Renaissance, Italy 1460-1500*, tr. Griffin, Thames & Hudson 1966

Albert Châtelet: *Van Eyck*, Bologna 1979

Herschel B. Chipp, ed. *Theories of Modern Art*, University Press of California, Los Angeles 1968

J.E. Cirlot. *A Dictionary of Symbols*, Routledge, London, 1981

Kenneth Clark: *Rembrandt and the Italian Renaissance*, John Murray 1969

Bruce Cole: *The Renaissance Artist at Work*, John Murray 1983

—. *Piero della Francesca: Tradition and Innovation in Renaissance Art*, Harper Collins, New York 1991

J.C. Cooper. *An Illustrated Dictionary of Traditional Symbols*, Thames & Hudson, London, 1978

Pierre Courthion: *Flemish Painting*, Thames & Hudson 1958

Paul Crossley: "Medieval Architecture and Meaning: The Limits of Iconography", *Burlington Magazine*, CXXX, 1988

Charles D. Cuttler: *Northern Painting From Pucelle to Bruegel*, Holt, Rineheart & Winston, New York 1968

Martin Davies: *Rogier van der Weyden*, Phaidon 1972

—. *The Early Netherlandish School*, London 1968

Valentin Denis: *Tutta la pittura di Jan van Eyck*, Milan 1954

Elisabeth Dhanens: *Hubert and Jan van Eyck*, New York 1980

G. Didi-Huberman: *Fra Angelico. Dissemblance et Figuration*, Flammarion, Paris 1990

Lene Dresen-Coenders, ed: *Saints and She-Devils: Images of Women in the 15th and 16th Centuries*, Rubicon Press 1987

Andrea Dworkin: *Pornography: Men Possessing Women*, Women's Press 1984

Donald Ehresmann: "Some Observations on the Role of the Liturgy in the Early Winged Altarpiece", *Art Bulletin*, LXIV, 1982

Colin Eisler: *Early Netherlandish Painting: The Thyssen-Bornemisza Collection*, Sotheby's Publications 1989

Mircea Eliade: *Ordeal by Labyrinth*, University of Chicago Press 1984

—. *A History of Religious Ideas*, I, Collins 1979

—. *Patterns in Comparative Religion*, Sheed & Ward 1958

—. *Symbolism, the Sacred and the Arts*, Crossroad, New York 1985

Joan Evans, ed: *The Flowering of the Middle Ages*, Thames & Hudson 1966

Giorgio T. Faggin: *The Complete Paintings of the Van Eycks*, Wiedenfeld & Nicolson 1970

R.L. Falkenberg: *Joachim Patinir: Landscape as an Image of the Pilgrimage of Life*, Amsterdam 1988

George Ferguson: *Signs and Symbols in Christian Art*, Oxford University

Press 1961

John Ferguson: *An Illustrated Encyclopaedia of Mysticism,* Thames & Hudson 1976

Peter Fingesten: *The Eclipse of Symbolism*, University Press of California 1970

John Fletcher & Andrew Benjamin, ed; *Abjection, Melancholia and Love: the Work of Julia Kristeva*, Routledge 1990

S.J. Freedberg: *Painting of the High Renaissance in Rome and Florence*, Harper & Row, New York 1972

Max J. Friedlander: *From Van Eyck to Bruegel*, Phaidon 1969

—. *The van Eycks, Petrus Christus, Early Netherlandish Painting*, vol. 1, tr. Heinz Norden, Sijthoff, Leyden, Netherlands 1967

—. *Hugo van der Goes: Early Netherlandish Painting*, vol. 4, tr. Heinz Norden, Sijthoff, Leyden, Netherlands 1967

—. *Memling*, Palet Series, 1949

Margaret Frinta: *The Genius of Robert Campin*, Paris 1966

Eugène Fromentin: *The Masters of Past Time: Dutch and Flemish Painting from Van Eyck to Rembrandt*, Phaidon 1981

Fred Gettings: *The Hidden Art: A Study of the Occult Symbolism in Art*, Studio Vista 1978

Matila Ghyka: *The Geometry of Art and Life*, Sheed & Ward, New York 1946

Marija Gimbutas: *The Language of the Goddess*, Thames & Hudson 1989

Carlo Ginzburg: *The Enigma of Piero: Piero della Francesca, The Baptism, The Arezzo Cycle, The Flagellation*, Verso 1985

F.M. Godfrey: *A Student's Guide to Italian Paintings 1250-1800*, Alec Tiranti 1965

Rona Goffen: *Giovanni Bellini*, Yale University Press, New Haven 1989

Robert Goldwater & Marco Treves, eds. *Artists on Art*, John Murray 1975

E.H. Gombrich: *Norm and Form: Studies in the Renaissance I*, Phaidon 1985

—. *Symbolic Images, Renaissance Studies II*, Phaidon 1985

Cecil Gould: *Leonardo: The Artist and the Non-Artist*, Weidenfeld & Nicholson 1975

—. "On the Direction of Light in Italian Renaissance Frescoes and Altarpieces", *Gazette des Beaux-Arts*, 6, XCVII, 1981

Rainald Grosshans: "Rogier van der Weyden, Der Marien altar aus der Kartäuse Miraflores", *Jahrbuch der Berliner Museen*, XXIII, 1981

John Hale: *Italian Renaissance Painting*, Phaidon 1977

James Hall: *A Dictionary of Subjects and Symbols in Art*, John Murray 1984

John Oliver Hand & Martha Wolff: *Early Netherlandish Painting*, National Gallery of Art, Washington DC 1986

F.C. Happold, ed. *Mysticism*, Penguin 1970

Craig Harbison: *Jan van Eyck: The Play of Realism*, Reaktion Books, 1991

—. "Realism and Symbolism and Art-historical Method", *Simiolus*, XIX, 1989

—. "Visions and Meditations in Early Flemish Painting", *Simiolus*, XV, 1985

Frederick Hartt: *History of Italian Renaissance Art: Painting, Sculpture, Architecture*, Thames & Hudson 1987

—. *Sandro Botticelli*, Collins 1954

Annemarie Vels Heijn: *Rembrandt*, tr. Weir, Scala Books 1969

P. Hendy: *Piero della Francesca and the Early Renaissance*, London 1968

Hans Hoftsatter: *Art of the Late Middle Ages*, Abrams, New York 1968

D. Hollanders-Favart & R. van Schouteeds: *Le Dessin sous-jacent dans la peinture, Le Problème Maître de Flémalle–van der Weyden*, Louvain-la-Neuve, 1981

William Hood: *Fra Angelico at San Marco*, Yale University Press, New Haven 1993

Michael Jacobs: *A Guide to European Painting*, David & Charles 1980

Charles Johnson: *Memlinc*, Faber, n.d.

Penny Howell Jolly: "Rogier van der Weyden's Escorial and Philadelphia *Crucifixions* and their relation to Fra Angelico at San Marco", *Oud Holland*, XCV, 1981, 113-126

Diane Kelder: *Pageant of the Renaissance*, Pall Mall Press 1969

Julia Kristeva: *The Kristeva Reader*, ed. Toril Moi, Blackwell 1986

—. *Desire in Language: A Semiotic Approach to Literature and Art*, ed. Leon Roudiez, tr. Thomas Gora, Alice Jardine & Leon Roudiez, Blackwell 1982

—. *Tales of Love*, tr. Leon S. Roudiez, Columbia University Press, New York 1987

Weston La Barre: *The Ghost Dance*, Allen & Unwin 1972

Barbara Lane: *The Altar and the Altarpiece: Sacramental Themes in Early Netherlandish Painting*, New York 1984

—. "Sacred vs Profane in Early Netherlandish Painting", *Simiolus*, XVIII, 1988

Robert Lawlor: *Sacred Geometry: Philosophy and Practice*, Thames & Hudson 1984

Leonardo da Vinci: *Selections from the Notebooks*, Oxford University Press 1952

Michael Levey: *High Renaissance*, Penguin 1975

—. *Early Renaissance*, Penguin 1967

Christopher Lloyd: *Fra Angelico*, Phaidon 1979

—. *A Picture History of Art*, Phaidon 1979

Robert Longhi: *Piero della Francesca,* Milan 1955

K.B. MacFarlane: *Hans Memling*, Clarendon Press 1971

Emile Male: *The Gothic Image*, Collins 1961

Elaine Marks & Isabelle de Courtivron, eds: *New French Feminisms: an Anthology*, Har-vester Wheatsheaf 1981

G. Marchini: *Filippo Lippi*, Electa Editrice, Milan 1975

James Marrow: "Symbol and Meaning in Northern European Art of the Late Middle Ages and Early Renaissance", *Simiolus*, XVI, 1986

Christine Hasenmueller McCorkel: "The role of the suspended Crown in Jan van Eyck's *Madonna and Chancellor Rolin*", *Art Bulletin*, LVIII, 1975

K.B. MacFarlane. *Hans Memling*, Clarendon Press, Oxford, 1971

M.B. McNamee: "The Origins of the Vested Angel as a Eucharistic Symbol in Flemish Painting" *Art Bulletin*, LIV, 1972

Milliard Meiss: "Light as Form and Symbol in Some Fifteenth Century Paintings", *Art Bulletin*, XXVII, 1945

J.C.J. Metford: *Dictionary of Christian Lore and Legend,* Thames & Hudson 1983

Toril Moi: *Sexual/Textual Politics: Feminist Literary Theory*, Routledge 1988

Edward Mullins: *The Painted Witch: Female Body, Male Art*, Secker & Warburg 1985

Peter & Linda Murray: *The Penguin Dictionary of Art and Artists*, Penguin 1976

Linda Murray: *High Renaissance*, Thames & Hudson 1977

Lawrence Naftulin: "A Note on the Iconography of the van der Paele Madonna", *Oud-Holland*, LXXXVI, 1971

Lynda Nead: *Female Nude: Art, Obscenity and Sexuality*, Routledge 1992

Erich Neumann: *The Great Mother*, Princeton University Press, New Jersey 1972

Shirley Nicholson, ed. *The Goddess Re-awakening: The Goddess Principle Today* Theosophical Publishing House, New York 1989

Rudolf Otto: *The Idea of the Holy*, Oxford University Press 1958

Otto Pächt: *Van Eyck and the Founders of Early Netherlandish Painting*, Harvey Miller 1994

Erwin Panofsky: *Studies in Iconology*, Harper & Row, New York 1972

—. *Early Netherlandish Painting*, Harvard University Press, Mass., 1953

Geoffrey Parrinder: *Mysticism in the World's Religions,* Sheldon Press 1976

Walter Pater: *The Renaissance*, Oxford University Press 1980

Michael Payne: *Reading Theory: An Introduction to Lacan, Derrida, and*

Kristeva, Blackwell 1993

Robert Payne: *Leonardo da Vinci*, Robert Hale 1979

Karen Petersen & J.J. Wilson: *Women Artists: Recognition and Reappraisal from the Early Middle Ages to the Twentieth Century* Women's Press, 1978

Lotte Brand Philip: *The Ghent Altarpiece and the Art of Jan van Eyck*, Princeton University Press 1971

J. Plummer & I. Lavin, eds: *Studies in Late Medieval and Renaissance Painting Presented to Millard Meiss*, New York University Press, New York 1977

Piero della Francesca: *The Complete Paintings of Piero della Francesca*, intr. Peter Murray, notes by Pierluigi de Vecchi, Penguin, 1985

John Pope-Hennessy: *Fra Angelico*, Phaidon 1974

Mario Praz: *The Romantic Agony, tr.* Davidson, Oxford University Press 1933

Carol Purtle: *The Marian Paintings of Jan van Eyck*, Princeton University Press, Princeton 1982

Leo van Puyvelde: *Flemish Painting From the Van Eycks to Metsys*, tr. Alan Kendall, Weidenfeld & Nicolson 1970

Carlo Ludovico Ragghianti, ed: *Great Museums of the World: Prado, Madrid*, Hamlyn 1969

D. Robb: "The Iconography of the Annunciation in the Fourteenth and Fifteenth Centuries", *Art Bulletin*, XVIII, 1936, 480-526

Jeremy Robinson: *Glorification: Religious Abstraction in Renaissance and 20th Century Painting*, Crescent Moon 1994

Heinz Roosen-Runge: *Die Rolin-Madonna des Jan van Eyck, Form und Inhalt*, Weisbaden 1972

Robert Rosenblum: *Modern Painting and the Northern Romantic Tradition*, Thames & Hudson 1978

Mark Roskill: *What is Art History?*, Thames & Hudson 1976

Peter H. Schabacker: *Petrus Christus*, Utrecht 1974

Wolfgang Schöne: *Dieric Bouts und seine Schule*, Berlin 1938

Anne Markham Schulz: "The Columba Altarpiece and Rogier van der Weyden's Stylistic Development", *Münchener Jahrbuch der bildenden Kunst*, 3rd series, XX, 1971

Larry Silver: "Fountain and Source: A Rediscovered Eyckian Icon", *Pantheon*, XLI, 1983

Alistair Smith: *Early Netherlandish and German Painting*, National Gallery 1985

Molly Teasdale Smith: "On the Donor of Jan van Eyck's Rolin Madonna", *Gesta*, XX, 1981

James Snyder: "Jan van Eyck and the Madonna of Chancellor Nicolas Rolin", *Oud-Holland*, LXXXII, 1967

Micheline Sonke & J. Folie: *Het werk van Rogier de la Pasture Van der Weyden*, Tournai 1964

J. Spencer: "Spatial Imagery of the Annunciation in Fifteenth-century Florence", *Art Bulletin*, XXXVI, 1955, 273-280

Sidney Spencer: *Mysticism in World Religion*, Penguin 1963

Oswald Spengler: *The Decline of the West*, ed. H. Werner, Allen & Unwin 1962

Wolfgang Stechow: *Northern Renaissance Art, 1400-1600, Sources and Documents*, Prentice-Hall, New Jersey 1966

L. Steinberg & S. Edgerton: "How shall this be? Reflections on Filippo Lippi's *Annunciation* in London", *Artibus et Historiae*, VIII, 1987, 25-53

Frank Stella: *Working Space,* Harvard University Press, Cambridge, Mass., 1986

Charles Sterling: "Observations on Petrus Christus", *Art Bulletin*, LIII, 1971

Victor I. Stoichita: *Leonardo da Vinci*, Abbey Library 1978

Peter Streider: *Dürer: Paintings, Prints, Drawings*, F. Muller 1982

Ruth Massey Tovell: *Rogier van der Weyden and the Flémalle Enigma*, Burns & MacEachern, 1955

Patrick Trevor-Roper: *The world blunted through sight: An inquiry into the influence of defective vision on art and character*, Thames & Hudson 1970

Walter Ueberwasser: *Rogier van der Weyden: Paintings From the Escorial and the Prado Museum*, B.T. Batsford, 1947

J.M. Upton: *Petrus Christus*, University Park 1990

Nicholas Usherwood: *The Bible in 20th Century Art*, Pagoda Books 1987

Lionello Venturi: *Renaissance Painting, from Leonardo to Dürer*, Skira/ Macmillan 1979

—. *Italian Paintings,* Zwemmer 1950

—. *Botticelli*, Phaidon 1964

T. Verdon & J. Henderson, eds: *Christianity and the Renaissance*, Syracuse University Press, Syracuse 1990

W. Vogelsang: *Rogier van der Weyden's Pietà,* Longmans, Green & Co, 1949

John Ward: "A New Attribution for the *Madonna Enthroned* in the Thyssen-Bornemisza Collection", *Art Bulletin*, L, 1968

—. "Hidden Symbolism in Jan van Eyck's Annunciations", *Art Bulletin*, LVII, 1975

Marina Warner: *Alone Of All Her Sex: The Myth and Cult of the Virgin Mary*, Picador 1985

—. *Monuments and Maidens,* Weidenfeld & Nicholson 1985

Paul Watson: *The Garden of Love in Tuscan Art of the Early Renaissance,* Associated University Press 1979

Margaret Whinney: *Early Flemish Painters,* Faber 1966

John White: *The Birth and Rebirth of Pictorial Space,* Faber 1957/87

Edward C. Whitmont: *Return of the Goddess,* Routledge 1987

Peter Lamborn Wilson: *Angels,* Thames & Hudson 1980

Mara R. Witzling: *Voicing Our Viions: Writing by Women Artists,* Women's Press 1992

Heinrich Wolfflin: *Classic Art,* Phaidon 1952/80

Marion Woodman: *The Pregnant Virgin: A Process of Psychological Transformation,* Inner City Books, Toronto 1989

Manfred Wudram: *Art of the Renaissance,* Weidenfeld & Nicolson 1985

J.E. Zeigler: "The Medieval Virgin as Object: Art of Anthropology?", *Historical Reflections,* XVI, 1989

Charles Zika: "Hosts, Processions and Pilgrimages: Controlling the Sacred in Fifteenth-Century Germany", *Past and Present,* CXVIII, 1988

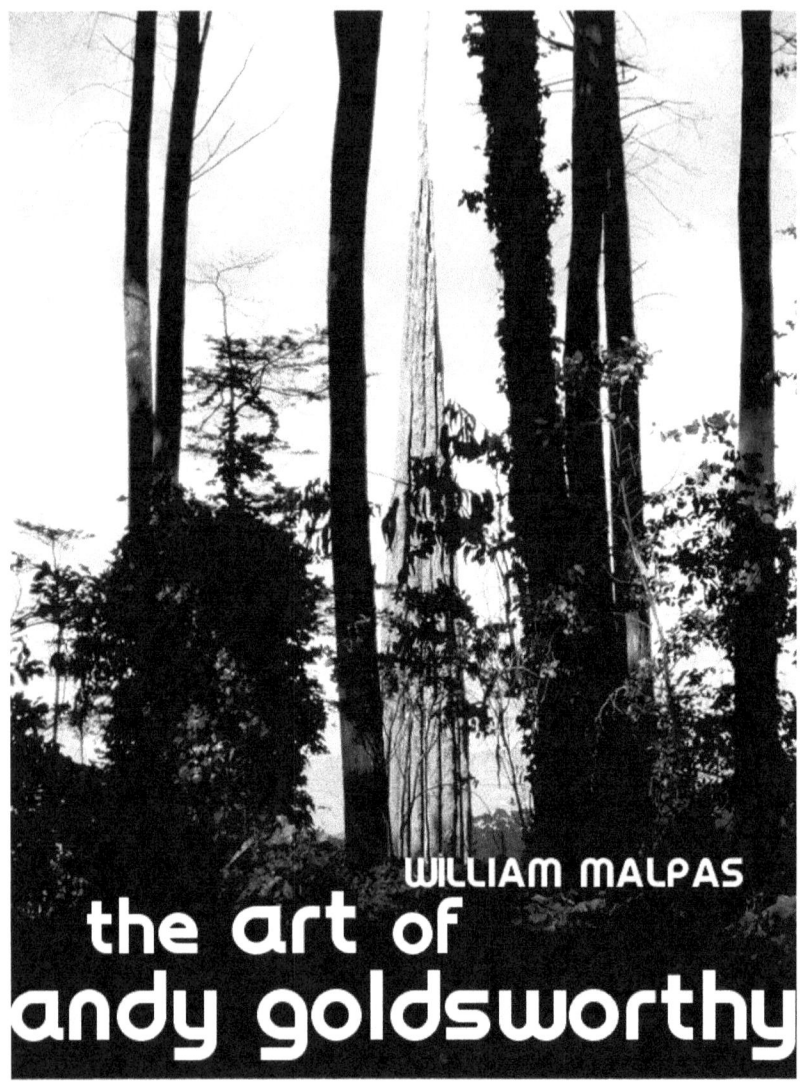

WILLIAM MALPAS
the art of
andy goldsworthy

This is the most comprehensive and detailed account of the art of Andy Goldsworthy available.

This study of Andy Goldsworthy discusses all of Goldsworthy's major exhibitions, books and projects, including the *Sheepfolds* project; *Garden of Stones* in New York; TV and dance collaborations; and the books *Wood*, *Stone*, *Time* and *Passage*. William Malpas surveys all of Goldsworthy's output, and analyzes his relation with other land artists such as Robert Smithson, the Christos, Walter de Maria, Chris Drury, Richard Long and David Nash; women sculptors; sculpture in the modern era; and Goldsworthy's place in the contemporary British art scene.

The book has been updated and revised for this new edition.

ISBN 9781861714107 Pbk   ISBN 9781861714114 Hbk
Fully illustrated   www.crmoon.com

MAURICE SENDAK

& the art of children's book illustration

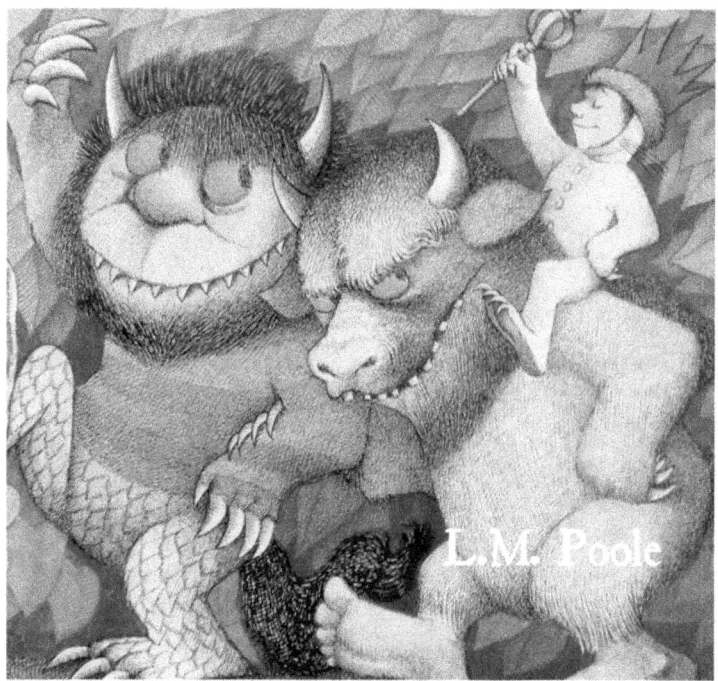

Maurice Sendak is the widely acclaimed American children's book author and illustrator. This critical study focuses on his famous trilogy, *Where the Wild Things Are,* *In the Night Kitchen* and *Outside Over There,* as well as the early works and Sendak's superb depictions of the Grimm Brothers' fairy tales in *The Juniper Tree.* L.M. Poole begins with a chapter on children's book illustration, in particular the treatment of fairy tales. Sendak's work is situated within the history of children's book illustration, and he is compared with many contemporary authors.

Fully illustrated. The book has been revised and updated for this edition.

ISBN 9781861714282 Pbk   ISBN 9781861713469 Hbk

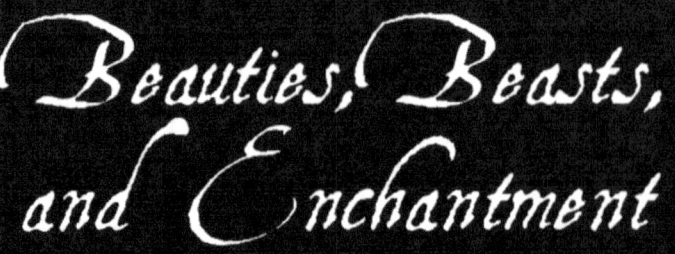

Beauties, Beasts, and Enchantment

CLASSIC FRENCH FAIRY TALES

Translated and with an Introduction
by Jack Zipes

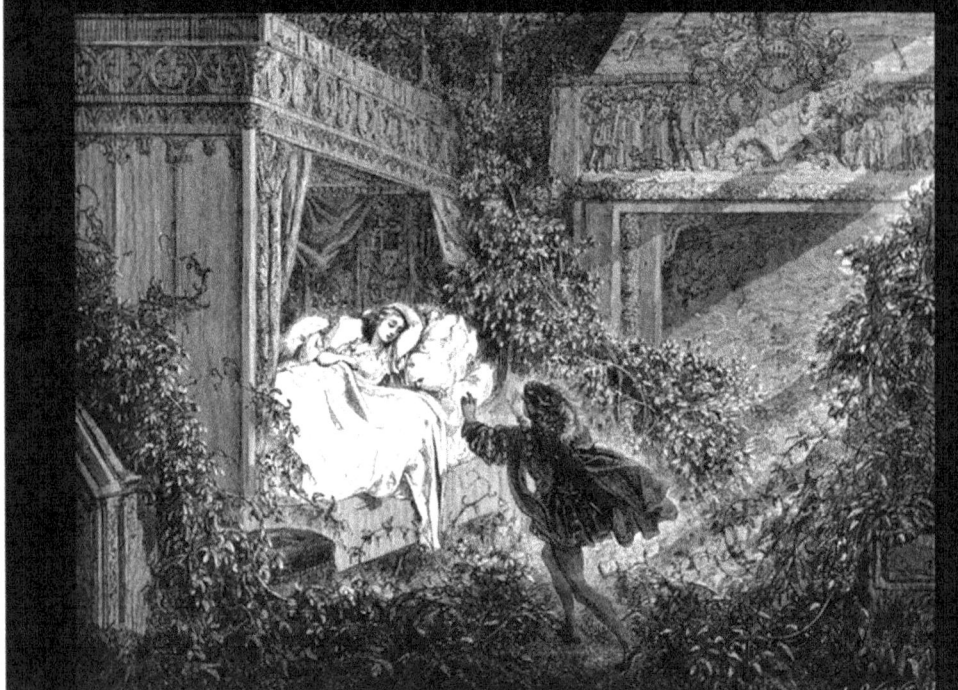

A collection of 36 classic French fairy tales translated by renowned writer Jack Zipes.
Cinderella, Beauty and the Beast, Sleeping Beauty and *Little Red Riding Hood* are among the
classic fairy tales in this amazing book.
Includes illustrations from fairy tale collections.
Jack Zipes has written and published widely on fairy tales.

'Terrific... a succulent array of 17th and 18th century 'salon' fairy tales'
- *The New York Times Book Review*

'These tales are adventurous, thrilling in a way fairy tales are meant to be... The translation
from the French is modern, happily free of archaic and hyperbolic language... a fine and
sophisticated collection' - *New York Tribune*

'Enjoyable to read... a unique collection of French regional folklore' - *Library Journal*

'Charming stories accompanied by attractive pen-and-ink drawings' - *Chattanooga Times*

Introduction and illustrations   612pp.   ISBN 9781861712510 Pbk   ISBN 9781861713193 Hbk

CRESCENT MOON PUBLISHING

web: www.crmoon.com e-mail: cresmopub@yahoo.co.uk

ARTS, PAINTING, SCULPTURE

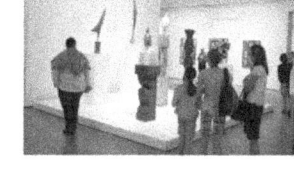
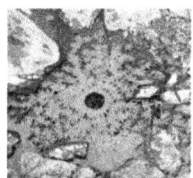
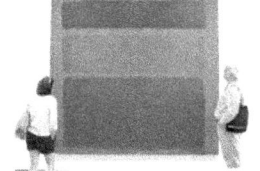

The Art of Andy Goldsworthy
Andy Goldsworthy: Touching Nature
Andy Goldsworthy in Close-Up
Andy Goldsworthy: Pocket Guide
Andy Goldsworthy In America
Land Art: A Complete Guide
The Art of Richard Long
Richard Long: Pocket Guide
Land Art In the UK
Land Art in Close-Up
Land Art In the U.S.A.
Land Art: Pocket Guide
Installation Art in Close-Up
Minimal Art and Artists In the 1960s and After
Colourfield Painting
Land Art DVD, TV documentary
Andy Goldsworthy DVD, TV documentary
The Erotic Object: Sexuality in Sculpture From Prehistory to the Present Day
Sex in Art: Pornography and Pleasure in Painting and Sculpture
Postwar Art
Sacred Gardens: The Garden in Myth, Religion and Art
Glorification: Religious Abstraction in Renaissance and 20th Century Art
Early Netherlandish Painting
Leonardo da Vinci
Piero della Francesca
Giovanni Bellini
Fra Angelico: Art and Religion in the Renaissance
Mark Rothko: The Art of Transcendence
Frank Stella: American Abstract Artist
Jasper Johns
Brice Marden
Alison Wilding: The Embrace of Sculpture
Vincent van Gogh: Visionary Landscapes
Eric Gill: Nuptials of God
Constantin Brancusi: Sculpting the Essence of Things
Max Beckmann
Caravaggio
Gustave Moreau
Egon Schiele: Sex and Death In Purple Stockings
Delizioso Fotografico Fervore: Works In Process 1
Sacro Cuore: Works In Process 2
The Light Eternal: J.M.W. Turner
The Madonna Glorified: Karen Arthurs

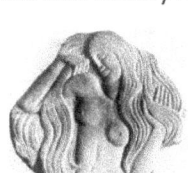
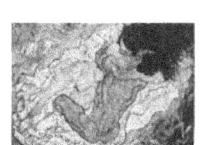
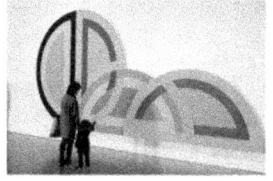
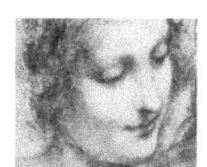
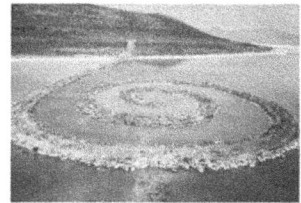

LITERATURE

J.R.R. Tolkien: The Books, The Films, The Whole Cultural Phenomenon
J.R.R. Tolkien: Pocket Guide
Tolkien's Heroic Quest
The *Earthsea* Books of Ursula Le Guin
Beauties, Beasts and Enchantment: Classic French Fairy Tales
German Popular Stories by the Brothers Grimm
Philip Pullman and *His Dark Materials*
Sexing Hardy: Thomas Hardy and Feminism
Thomas Hardy's *Tess of the d'Urbervilles*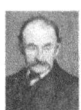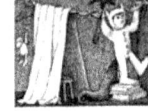
Thomas Hardy's *Jude the Obscure*
Thomas Hardy: The Tragic Novels
Love and Tragedy: Thomas Hardy
The Poetry of Landscape in Hardy
Wessex Revisited: Thomas Hardy and John Cowper Powys
Wolfgang Iser: Essays and Interviews
Petrarch, Dante and the Troubadours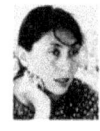
Maurice Sendak and the Art of Children's Book Illustration
Andrea Dworkin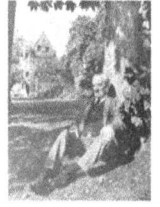
Cixous, Irigaray, Kristeva: The *Jouissance* of French Feminism
Julia Kristeva: Art, Love, Melancholy, Philosophy, Semiotics and Psychoanalysis
Hélène Cixous I Love You: The *Jouissance* of Writing
Luce Irigaray: Lips, Kissing, and the Politics of Sexual Difference
Peter Redgrove: Here Comes the Flood
Peter Redgrove: Sex-Magic-Poetry-Cornwall
Lawrence Durrell: Between Love and Death, East and West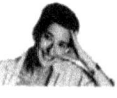
Love, Culture & Poetry: Lawrence Durrell
Cavafy: Anatomy of a Soul
German Romantic Poetry: Goethe, Novalis, Heine, Hölderlin
Feminism and Shakespeare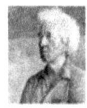
Shakespeare: Love, Poetry & Magic
The Passion of D.H. Lawrence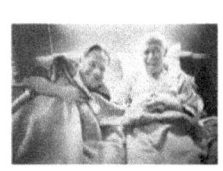
D.H. Lawrence: Symbolic Landscapes
D.H. Lawrence: Infinite Sensual Violence
Rimbaud: Arthur Rimbaud and the Magic of Poetry
The Ecstasies of John Cowper Powys
Sensualism and Mythology: The Wessex Novels of John Cowper Powys
Amorous Life: John Cowper Powys and the Manifestation of Affectivity (H.W. Fawkner)
Postmodern Powys: New Essays on John Cowper Powys (Joe Boulter)
Rethinking Powys: Critical Essays on John Cowper Powys
Paul Bowles & Bernardo Bertolucci
Rainer Maria Rilke
Joseph Conrad: *Heart of Darkness*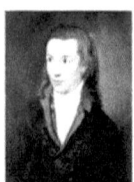
In the Dim Void: Samuel Beckett
Samuel Beckett Goes into the Silence
André Gide: Fiction and Fervour
Jackie Collins and the Blockbuster Novel
Blinded By Her Light: The Love-Poetry of Robert Graves
The Passion of Colours: Travels In Mediterranean Lands
Poetic Forms

POETRY

Ursula Le Guin: Walking In Cornwall
Peter Redgrove: Here Comes The Flood
Peter Redgrove: Sex-Magic-Poetry-Cornwall
Dante: Selections From the Vita Nuova
Petrarch, Dante and the Troubadours
William Shakespeare: Sonnets
William Shakespeare: Complete Poems
Blinded By Her Light: The Love-Poetry of Robert Graves
Emily Dickinson: Selected Poems
Emily Brontë: Poems
Thomas Hardy: Selected Poems
Percy Bysshe Shelley: Poems
John Keats: Selected Poems
Joh n Keats: Poems of 1820
D.H. Lawrence: Selected Poems
Edmund Spenser: Poems
Edmund Spenser: Amoretti
John Donne: Poems
Henry Vaughan: Poems
Sir Thomas Wyatt: Poems
Robert Herrick: Selected Poems
Rilke: Space, Essence and Angels in the Poetry of Rainer Maria Rilke
Rainer Maria Rilke: Selected Poems
Friedrich Hölderlin: Selected Poems
Arseny Tarkovsky: Selected Poems
Arthur Rimbaud: Selected Poems
Arthur Rimbaud: A Season in Hell
Arthur Rimbaud and the Magic of Poetry
Novalis: Hymns To the Night
German Romantic Poetry
Paul Verlaine: Selected Poems
Elizaethan Sonnet Cycles
D.J. Enright: By-Blows
Jeremy Reed: Brigitte's Blue Heart
Jeremy Reed: Claudia Schiffer's Red Shoes
Gorgeous Little Orpheus
Radiance: New Poems
Crescent Moon Book of Nature Poetry
Crescent Moon Book of Love Poetry
Crescent Moon Book of Mystical Poetry
Crescent Moon Book of Elizabethan Love Poetry
Crescent Moon Book of Metaphysical Poetry
Crescent Moon Book of Romantic Poetry
Pagan America: New American Poetry

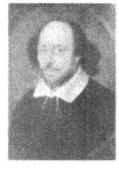
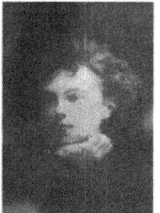
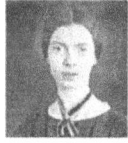
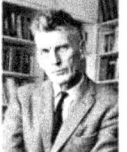
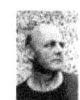
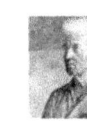
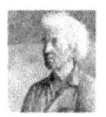
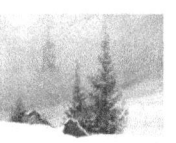
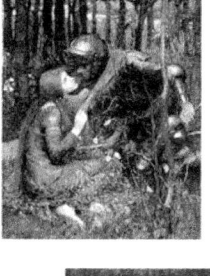
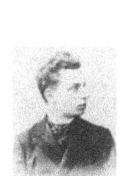
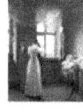
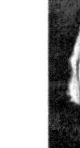
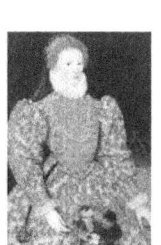

J.R.R. Tolkien: The Books, The Films, The Whole Cultural Phenomenon
J.R.R. Tolkien: Pocket Guide
The *Lord of the Rings* Movies: Pocket Guide
The Cinema of Hayao Miyazaki
Hayao Miyazaki: *Princess Mononoke*: Pocket Movie Guide
Hayao Miyazaki: *Spirited Away*: Pocket Movie Guide
Tim Burton : Hallowe'en For Hollywood
Ken Russell
Ken Russell: *Tommy*: Pocket Movie Guide
The Ghost Dance: The Origins of Religion
The Peyote Cult
Cixous, Irigaray, Kristeva: The *Jouissance* of French Feminism
Julia Kristeva: Art, Love, Melancholy, Philosophy, Semiotics and Psychoanalysis
Luce Irigaray: Lips, Kissing, and the Politics of Sexual Difference
Hélene Cixous I Love You: The *Jouissance* of Writing
Andrea Dworkin
'Cosmo Woman': The World of Women's Magazines
Women in Pop Music
HomeGround: The Kate Bush Anthology
Discovering the Goddess (Geoffrey Ashe)
The Poetry of Cinema
The Sacred Cinema of Andrei Tarkovsky
Andrei Tarkovsky: Pocket Guide
Andrei Tarkovsky: *Mirror*: Pocket Movie Guide
Andrei Tarkovsky: *The Sacrifice*: Pocket Movie Guide
Walerian Borowczyk: Cinema of Erotic Dreams
Jean-Luc Godard: The Passion of Cinema
Jean-Luc Godard: *Hail Mary*: Pocket Movie Guide
Jean-Luc Godard: *Contempt*: Pocket Movie Guide
Jean-Luc Godard: *Pierrot le Fou*: Pocket Movie Guide
John Hughes and Eighties Cinema
Ferris Bueller's Day Off: Pocket Movie Guide
Jean-Luc Godard: Pocket Guide
The Cinema of Richard Linklater
Liv Tyler: Star In Ascendance
Blade Runner and the Films of Philip K. Dick
Paul Bowles and Bernardo Bertolucci
Media Hell: Radio, TV and the Press
An Open Letter to the BBC
Detonation Britain: Nuclear War in the UK
Feminism and Shakespeare
Wild Zones: Pornography, Art and Feminism
Sex in Art: Pornography and Pleasure in Painting and Sculpture
Sexing Hardy: Thomas Hardy and Feminism

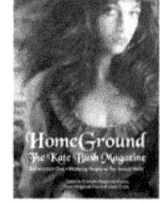
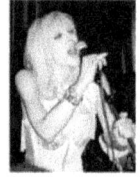
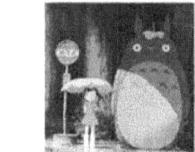
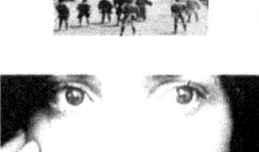

The Light Eternal is a model monograph, an exemplary job. The subject matter of the book is beautifully
organised and dead on beam. (Lawrence Durrell)
It is amazing for me to see my work treated with such passion and respect. (Andrea Dworkin)

CRESCENT MOON PUBLISHING
P.O. Box 1312, Maidstone, Kent, ME14 5XU, Great Britain. www.crmoon.com

cresmopub@yahoo.co.uk   www.crescentmoon.org.uk

www.ingramcontent.com/pod-product-compliance
Lightning Source LLC
Chambersburg PA
CBHW051324220526
45468CB00004B/1482